PLANT
POWERED

Published in the UK in 2021 by Plant Powered Publishing

Paperback ISBN 978-1-8383407-0-4
.epub eBook 978-1-8383407-1-1
.mobi eBook ISBN 978-1-8383407-2-8

Cover design and typeset by Spiffing Covers

TRANSFORM YOUR BODY AND OUR PLANET BY GOING

PLANT POWERED

ADAM STANSBURY

Contents

DISCLAIMER

The content of this book should not be considered a substitute for professional medical advice or expertise.

Please speak to your GP, a qualified nutritionist or dietitian before you make any lifestyle, nutritional or dietary changes.

I am not a qualified dietician or nutritionist but I do have multiple fitness industry coaching qualifications along with:

Over 20 years of personal experience (since 1999) taking my body through many transformations, ranging from fitness modelling, traumatic illness, lifesaving abdominal surgery, bodybuilding shows and photo shoots.

Over 10 years of profession personal training experience (since 2009) transforming the bodies and lives of hundreds of clients on and offline, applying what I've learnt, and replicating the results in the real world both as a meat eater and as a vegan.

Over 5 years of vegan personal and professional coaching experience (since 2014), I have gone on the journey 'from meat to plants' myself and have coached many clients to make the transition themselves to a plant-based diet.

You can see that this level of personal and professional experience on both sides of the fence puts me in a unique position to dispel many of the myths the media would like you to believe when it comes to eating plants, but mainstream media is now starting to talk more openly about the benefits of a plant-based diet, which is a sign of the changing times.

What you read in this book has been tried and tested, it's not just based on scientific studies or texts from other books, it's based on actual real-world personal and professional experiences and observations.

ACKNOWLEDGEMENTS

I prefer to call this my 'Gratitude List' because it is truly a list of all the people I am grateful for that have supported me through my life, career and ultimately the realisation of this, my first book.

This list must start from the top and where it all began.

My mother who has always been there for me through sunshine and rain, supporting me, loving me and taking care of me through illness and celebrating me in life. Words are not enough. I was a very lucky soul to have you as a Mother, thank you Mum, I love you.

My father who has become, much later in life, one of my biggest supporters and the biggest supporter of this book project. Your wisdom, support and guidance was so appreciated through the failure of crowdfunding and again your support through the self-publishing process has meant so much to me, as has our deepening relationship and friendship as we've both grown older and travelled further down this life journey together, I love you very much.

Thank you, to you both, for supporting me down the unconventional life path I chose and the headaches it may have caused along the way.

My brother who I fought hard with when I was a kid over sweets and toys, amongst many other things, but who has been one of my greatest supporters later in life and who has dropped pearls of wisdom during some very difficult times that changed the course of my life. I love the fact you have also chosen the road less travelled and I think that's where our deep love and respect for each other later in life has come from.

To all my friends who I have shared many deep and meaningful moments with and mind shatteringly fun, meaningless moments with over the years; our conversations and times together have helped shape me and my thoughts. I won't single you out, as you have all had an impact on my life, you know who you are and you know what we have shared, I love you.

Thanks to my ex-wife, Steph, who supported me in the early days of this book's journey. For watching me speak at that first Vevolution event and also as I put pen to paper and wrote the manuscript back in Summer 2018, thank you, I'll always love you.

To my Personal Training mentors over the years Dan Boulle, David Petersen and Simon Jeffery that forged me into the coach I am today, your passion for the industry set mine on fire and has carried me to this far.

A special thanks to Simon for, without your encouragement and inspiration, I would never have entered and ultimately won Personal Trainer of the Year in 2013.

Thanks to Damien and Judy Clarkson who helped inspire and guide me on my early journey into the vegan world and community and who gave me the opportunities to speak at the Vevolution events that started the ball rolling with my presentations and this book.

To Robbie and Klaus at Plant Based News for supporting me, to Cem Yildiz, Loui Blake and Tom McGillycuddy for being inspirational plant-powered friends and entrepreneurs, that I have had the pleasure of watching as your businesses have grown so successfully.

Rich Roll, you haven't met me yet, but you have been a big hero and inspiration for my plant-powered journey since 2014, maybe one day we will meet, thank you.

A huge, deep heartfelt thank you to Joanna, my love, my life partner, my best friend since 2007 and supporter of not only my work, but of me. You see me, understand me, support me and laugh with me through the challenges that life throws at us and the absolute pure bliss and joy that we experience together each day on this life journey, I love you very much.

Thank you to Mother Ayahuasca, the 'Vine of the Soul', for reconnecting me with my true nature and for showing me the magic that exists beyond the veil of this physical reality.

And finally, thank you to Mother Nature, Gaia, The Universe, God, Spirit, whatever label you wish to give to the energetic infrastructure that informs all manifestation and allows me to have this wonderful experience we call life.

THIS BOOK

Is split into three parts:

Part 1 – Becoming Plant Powered
This part is about my journey from meat to plants, the observations I've made, the philosophy behind my decisions and practical advice to help you with your own plant-powered journey.

Part 2 – Plant-Powered Fitness
This part covers the philosophy and practical steps behind goal setting, fitness training and nutrition to improve health, body composition and performance on a plant-based diet.

Part 3 – Protein and Our Planet
This part explores the rise in popularity of the fitness industry, our obsession with animal protein and what affect this is having on our relationship with the planet, the environment and each other.

WHO IS THIS BOOK FOR?

Are you becoming increasingly conscious of the food you are eating, what it contains and where it originates? or are you curious about switching to a plant-based diet? This book will support a range of people curious about making more conscious food choices, created from the experience I have gained over the years through my professional advice and services.

The Conscious Fitness Enthusiasts

You may want to transition away from eating meat to a plant-based diet but feel stuck in the fitness world's obsessive approach to animal protein. Are you starting to question your food choices but want to know how to preserve performance and physical health, while adopting more conscious food choices?

The Veggie to Vegan

Have you been vegetarian for years but now see not only the health impact of consuming dairy but the ethical and environmental reasons for letting go of dairy from your life?

The Want-To-Be-Fitter Vegan

Are you vegan, but haven't quite yet been able to get into the physical shape you desire? You are aware of the ethics, but just need inspiring, practical, performance-related training and nutrition advice. Part 2 will be of specific interest to you.

The Inquisitive

Are you inquisitive as to what a plant-based diet is all about?
Are you looking for inspiration?
Are you open to learning more?

Perhaps you're ready for a new way of seeing nutrition or maybe you have begun to question the amount of animal protein you're eating and the effects those choices are having on the world.

I've written this book to resolve many of the mistruths and misunderstandings that are out there concerning a plant-based diet, its impact on health, fitness and our planet. It's time we stopped isolating each one and started understanding that everything is connected.

PROLOGUE

Health and fitness for me used to be about getting into the best physical shape possible, whatever the cost. When I trained for the first two or three fitness shows I lived a 'hermit' lifestyle, living in fear of food outside of my programme. I feared social occasions when the menu would be out of my control and could affect all the obsessive eating and training I was doing just to get my body into the leanest shape possible, to look good on stage. The more the physical body became my focus, the more obsessive and unhealthier it became – and still does – unless it is balanced with health, function and a broader view of the world.

As this life journey goes on and the more injuries, rehabs and recoveries my body has gone through, there is the realisation that while I still want my body to look great with good muscle definition, my priority has shifted away from just aesthetics and more towards function, health and longevity. Looking good is all well and good but I want to live longer with good enough health and physical functionality to enjoy life and I hope that this wonderful planet we live on lasts long enough for you, me and many generations to come to experience it.

When I ate meat and competed in fitness shows my focus was on buying and eating low-cost meat so I could afford to hit the excessive protein requirements I felt I needed. During those times I became obsessed about my body and was blind to everything else, with no awareness of where that meat was coming from and the effects it was having, not just on my health, but the health of animals and that of the environment.

The switch to eating more plants gave my body and life the balance it needed in terms of health, performance, body composition and a deeper awareness of the cycle of life around me.

Leading a life that has been both excessive and obsessive in the past, has allowed me to now find balance, opening my eyes and providing me with the mission of this book.

"I can only experience what I am,
by experiencing what I am not."
(Conversations with God *by Neale Donald Walsch)*

You can obtain a body that looks good on the outside, is optimised for health and longevity on the inside and that works in harmony with nature and our environment in a way that reduces trauma and suffering.

This book has been formulated thanks to over 40 years of life experience and crafted in the fires of many public-speaking presentations, festivals, events and workshops that helped me combine my story, knowledge, experience, recipes and purpose into a powerful and engaging message that I'm very passionate about, which is always evolving as am I.

Unbeknown to me at the time, those talks and presentations were a great testing ground for my message. After each event I would tweak the presentation and take on board the feedback I received to improve it. This process gave me the confidence to sit down and put it all into a much more detailed format and into a book that I know will resonate with many people.

This book will help those starting their plant-powered journeys with trustworthy and authentic information and philosophy, based on science, observation, and personal experience, from my lifelong journey and passion for food, philosophy and fitness. Each chapter also provides you with a thoughtful quote to ponder and a plant-powered recipe to try as we make our way through the book and our journey together.

At the end of the day I just want to reduce the trauma and suffering that I leave in the wake of my life on this planet, which I feel permeates into all other areas of human life.

I hope that after reading this book you will also feel driven to express more empathy, compassion and love for animals, the environment and each other.

Vevolution Topics 2017 – Where my plant-powered public speaking began...

INTRODUCTION

Rather than dwelling on individual trees,
we must examine the shape of the forest.

Veganism isn't perfect. Nothing on our planet works 100% of the time for 100% of the people, but 80% plant based is better than nothing at all.

We need to move beyond the constant arguments comparing different diets and the biased studies to back up their health benefits for the individual. If we know there are a few different ways of eating that can benefit people's health, then surely we need to expand the arguments and consideration beyond just the impact the food we eat has on our own bodies and start becoming more aware of the impact those choices make on the world around us.

The global fitness industry is rapidly expanding and worth over $83 billion, helped by the global influence of social media where (at the time of writing) hashtags such as #Fitness on Instagram have over 420 million posts. Yet the cost for treating obesity is set to top $1.2 trillion every year from 2025.

Alongside the lust for the body beautiful and the need to pack on muscle, comes an ever-increasing need for protein, protein that is mostly derived from animals.

Over 74 billion land animals are slaughtered every year with animal agriculture responsible for anything between 18–50% of all global greenhouse gas emissions. Livestock now uses 30% of the Earth's entire ice-free land surface, with another 33% of arable land used for feed crop production, turning our beautiful and naturally diverse planet into a gigantic farm.

Climate change is now at the forefront of everyone's minds, with rising CO_2 levels not only increasing global warming but reducing the nutrient quality of our plants, soil and food.

There is something worrying about a world that chooses to eat vast quantities of animal products to satisfy their taste buds and physical goals, while disregarding the misery, trauma and suffering we inflict on farmed animals and the damage caused to vital ecosystems. And all because of the misguided beliefs that animal protein is superior to plant protein and that it is needed in the quantities we have been led to believe.

But it doesn't have to be that way. The plant-based movement is now on the rise as people start to realise the negative health, ethical and environmental costs that eating a diet heavy in animal products can incur, and the host of benefits that come with eating a plant-based diet.

1. Do we need to get our protein from animal sources?
2. Can plants provide all the essential nutrients that we require?
3. Where has this protein obsession come from and is it necessary?

4. What effect is this protein obsession having on our health, animals and the planet?

These are just a few of the questions I intend to answer throughout my book.

Plant Powered will show you how to transform YOUR body and OUR planet just by changing the food choices you make.

THE THREE PRINCIPLES OF PLANT POWER

These principles are the bedrock of my ethos and mission behind living a life that is plant powered, the coaching that I provide and the book you are now reading.

1. Reduce Trauma and Suffering

The first principle is the foundation and the reason why I adopted a plant-based diet – not specifically for health, but for ethics and morality. Following a plant-based diet by definition leads us towards a future that focuses on reducing the amount of trauma and suffering that our lives lead behind. This is the main principle I encourage others to follow, as it is, I believe, the most black and white reason for following a plant-based diet. It will give you a strong enough WHY, that will carry you through and guide the more difficult and challenging choices that you make.

We now live in a world that has given us the freedom to live, eat and think this way. If we were still in the 'wild' it may not be quite as easy, so if we have the luxury of this choice, why wouldn't we make it?

2. Progress Not Perfection

Change will come about far quicker when billions of people strive for progress rather than thousands that strive for perfection, which is also an unrealistic goal for imperfect humans. Striving for perfection – to live the perfect life, to eat the perfect diet – will only pile pressure onto your shoulders that will burn you out and leave you feeling like a failure when you are unable to achieve such unattainable heights, often too soon in your journey.

We are constantly evolving beings, physically, mentally, spiritually and philosophically.

This is a principle that I wholeheartedly encourage all my clients to adopt when embarking on the journey of self-optimisation through plant-based nutrition and exercise. The journey is long, it has no ultimate destination, although you may believe it does. I have taken my body on many transformations over the years and each time I believed 'this is the one', only to realise that there would be a new goal, a new process and a new destination around the corner.

Focus on just being a better version of yourself and having NO ZERO DAYS!

3. Simple = Sustainable

Over-complicating the way you approach any goal in life will provide you with far too many opportunities to slip up and 'fall off the wagon' and relapse on your current change cycle. If you follow a simple plan that has fewer actionable points, you are far more likely to complete each one, providing you with the sustainability that is needed in order to achieve your goals.

A simple approach will allow you to make progress more frequently, inching you ever closer towards improving – not perfecting – yourself and your situation.

PART 1

BECOMING PLANT POWERED

CHAPTER 1

MY JOURNEY

"You never know how strong you are, until being strong is the only choice you have."
BOB MARLEY

My name is Adam Stansbury and I am The Plant Powered PT. My mission is to get men and women fit, strong and healthy on a plant-based diet, while raising their consciousness and providing a deeper connection to who they are and the world around them, but it hasn't always been that way.

I was an avid meat eater for the first 36 years of my life, finally 'seeing the light' and making the transition to a plant-based diet in November 2014. This is, was and continues to be a pivotal part of my life journey and mission. It's about more than just food, it's about leading a more conscious and compassionate life.

Proteinaholic

I was a self-confessed 'Proteinaholic', eating rib-eye steak, lamb steaks or burgers for breakfast on a regular basis, several chicken breasts throughout the day, fish for dinner and washing it all down with whey protein shakes.

I was a product of the fitness industry and bodybuilding world's obsession with protein, or more specifically, animal protein, because like most I believed plant protein was inferior.

I regularly sacrificed the quality of the meat that I ate just so I could financially ensure all six of my daily meals contained some form of animal protein that would support my muscular gains and help me avoid losing all that muscle I'd worked so hard for in the gym.

Many Sunday evenings were spent bagging up portions of chicken breasts and beef mince into freezer bags, from huge 6–10kg tubs of meat bought from the local cash and carry.

I never once considered the effect this might be having, or had, on my own health, let alone the trauma and suffering inflicted on the animals who had died to supply me with their flesh and to support my muscle-building lifestyle. At the time I also had no idea of the detrimental effect animal agriculture was having on the natural world around me, of which I was playing my part in.

Ironic Beginnings

The start of my jouney is quite an ironic one, as I grew up in a small town called Trowbridge in Wiltshire, which is surrounded by many small rural towns, communities and villages. Wiltshire has some beautiful countryside, so it was quite common for many kids' families at school to own farms, many of whom turned out to be good friends of mine. I would spend many happy and long weekends on my friends' farms, getting up to mischief, playing around in nature, shooting things with air rifles, fishing and also witnessing the running of the farms.

My first job was definitely not vegan-friendly. Working in a butchers at the age of 16, I remember cleaning out the huge fridge freezers on a Saturday afternoon, stinking of bleach and blood, big carcasses of animals hanging around after being butchered. I didn't think much of it back then and I just got on with it. I never did any butchering, I was just there to clean, but I observed. I've been a pretty good observer all my life and here we are.

I was also an avid fisherman throughout my childhood. I loved the outdoors, nature, water and still have many fond memories of fishing adventures with friends. My angling obsession then took me to agricultural college to study fish farming.

It is these early childhood experiences of nature, animals and the suffering we cause to them that has built up within me over the years and has now manifested itself as this book. I couldn't have written this any earlier and I know all my past experiences have now led you and me to this point.

I was very sporty throughout my childhood and could usually be found outdoors with friends climbing trees, playing football, cricket or anything that required a degree of hand-eye coordination. In contrast, my brother, who is four years my senior, was usually found reading books and building model aircraft. Although he was not traditionally sporty like myself he loved the more adventurous pursuits of rock climbing, skiing and canoeing.

Although I was a very active child from the ages of about 11–15, I also carried around a degree of 'puppy fat' as most young boys and girls do, which I became quite self-conscious about. This was not helped when on one occasion my games teacher at school referred to me as 'fat and overweight' during an argument. Rather than let that bring me down it sent me the other way and I remember thinking, 'I'll never be the fat kid again'.

This was also the first time in my life that I turned a negative situation into a positive one and has been the cornerstone of how I have framed many of my subsequent life experiences.

Due to my naturally sporty nature and this new-found determination to improve my body, I was attracted at an early age to the impressive and inspirational images of men's physiques on the covers of magazines such as *Men's Health*, and the figures of Hollywood action heroes throughout the 80s such as Arnie, Sly Stallone, Jean Claude Van Dam and Dolph Lungren.

College

Considering the subject matter of this book and my chosen

When I came back from travelling, I decided to move up to Manchester to live with my girlfriend at the time. I was still working for the same company in Reading. They had been amazing at welcoming me back after my trip and gave me the opportunity to work remotely in a marketing capacity for them, with regular trips back down south to the Reading offices for meetings.

The relationship didn't last long and after we broke up I was encouraged by my travelling buddy Rob to try my luck at modelling, "while I still could" up in Manchester. So, at 25 I decided to visit Boss Model Management in Manchester to see what it was all about and to see if I could make the grade and genuinely start a career in modelling. It all seemed a bit far-fetched, but I thought I would give it a go.

At the time I was lifting weights more and more which had given me a bulkier look, but not giving much thought to strict dieting or cardiovascular work. I'd always hated cardio at school as I was carrying around a bit more weight and was built more for the shot-put rather than cross-country.

One of the bookers at the modelling agency must have felt she could see something beneath my chunky exterior as she asked me how long it would take to lose about a stone, and then to come back to the agency. I replied, "I'll be back in a month!"

This was the first time I witnessed two things. Firstly the blunt/honest approach taken by bookers at modelling agencies when handing out weight-loss advice to models; and secondly the combining of four important elements needed to improve body composition:

1. Setting a goal
2. Weight training
3. Cardiovascular training
4. Mindful eating

After carefully monitoring my nutrition intake and putting equal amounts of effort into the treadmill and the dumbbells, I stayed true to my word and returned to the modelling agency one month later and one stone lighter. They took me onto their books and booked me in for my first portfolio test shoot.

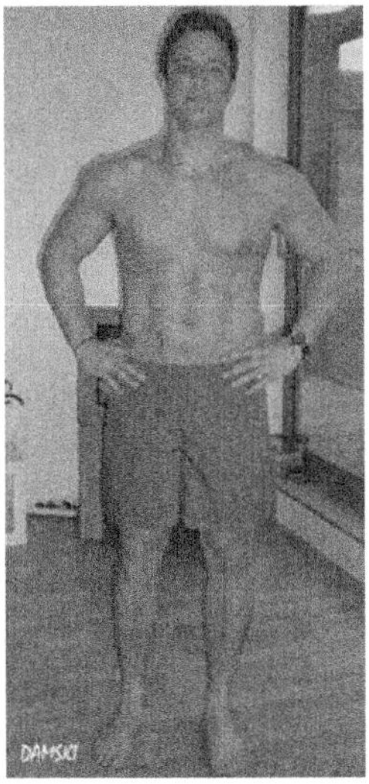

Stress and Illness

I was incredibly lucky to do some amazing photo shoots over the next few years, travelling to Florida for sportswear and football catalogue shoots on two different occasions, shooting men's catalogues in Palma, Mallorca, and travel brochures in Amsterdam, etc. But while there were some amazing high points in my modelling career – meeting great friends and going to great parties – much of the time was spent in poverty, debt and increasing anxiety about my limited cash flow. It was typically a champagne or baked beans lifestyle.

I managed to rack up some big debts on a couple of different credit cards as I waited for 'that job' that every model is waiting for and hears about on the grapevine. I was even put on option once for an alcohol commercial shooting in Italy worth 30,000 euros that never materialised, which would've fixed many of my debt worries at the time. That one big job is the 'carrot' that dangles in most models' faces for years and that keeps them in the game.

I'd stayed up north but had decided to move in with a friend in Liverpool, travelling backwards and forwards to castings in Manchester, but the modelling work became thinner on the ground and the less I worked, the more debt I built up on my credit cards and the more I worried.

Until one day after returning from Spain on a modelling job in early June 2005, I started to feel quite unwell and developed chronic stomach pain and diarrhoea. Looking back, I believe the illness that was about to take hold of me had been helped along by three main factors:

1. Stress and anxiety caused by my debt worries.
2. Bacterial infection while eating snails in Spain.
3. A heavy meat-based diet, that focused on quantity over quality.

Over the course of the next month I went back and forth to the local GP in Liverpool about four times, each time being sent away with a different pharmaceutical that would only ever help to relieve symptoms rather than help to fix the problem. Each time I knew in my heart that something more serious was going on inside me than indigestion and acid reflux, but no one seemed to be giving it any serious attention beyond prescribing me another drug.

On the final visit I demanded to be put in contact with a gastrointestinal specialist at the local hospital and was finally given an appointment on the NHS waiting list, in two months' time. There was no way I was going to be able to wait two months, especially as I was now bleeding out of my anus and in chronic pain every day. I was very lucky my mother stepped in and offered to pay for me to see a private specialist.

Six Packs Come and Go

You know your life is about to change when you're having an endoscopy (camera inserted into the anus) and the doctor takes one look on the screen showing the inside of your large intestine and says something along the lines of, "I've never seen that so bad in someone your age." Even in my drugged-up state I could see the damage and knew how serious it was.

That day I was diagnosed with UC (ulcerative colitis), which is the ulceration of the large intestine. I was also told two mistruths that could've prevented a cascade of traumatic experiences that were to come over the next two years and that have changed my life forever.

1. That it had nothing to do with nutrition.
2. The lining of the large intestine couldn't be repaired

I was given anti-inflammatory steroids and other medications to help keep everything manageable but was never given any guidance as to how I could heal or fix the problem and its potential root causes. So I just carried on with my life the way it had been, and for several months the medication actually helped keep everything in check, but it was only a matter of time before the 'dam' burst, because I was putting a 'band aid on a bullet wound.'

Modelling hadn't really improved much for me in Liverpool and I knew I had to make a bold move. So in November 2005 I decided to finally move back down south to London, and to try and make a go of this modelling thing. It would also bring me closer to family and a support network that it turned out I would be needing very soon.

Work really picked up for me as well to begin with. I moved in with friends, I was having a blast going out in London to model parties, I'd shot the cover for the *GNC* magazine (at the time *Healthy for Men*) In December 2005, I was in my best shape ever at the time and had a few thousand pounds worth of work booked in for the coming weeks. Then disaster struck.

In January 2006, while making a visit back up to Manchester for a modelling job and staying at a friend's place, I became very ill. It started during the photo shoot I was on, with debilitating flu-like symptoms that came on very quickly. I was lying on a sofa under a blanket in-between outfit changes, shivering manically.

Finally, I finished the job and made my way back into Manchester to stay at my friend's flat, feeling worse and worse by the minute and with a stomach that began to bloat out. We thought it was just flu but on the second day and at 3am in the morning with my stomach fully distended, and unable to keep any food or water down, we called an ambulance. I was taken to one of the big Manchester hospitals, where I was put on an antibiotic drip and given a bed.

After several tests and 48 hours later, the bloating had subsided and the doctors, although they had read my diagnosis from my appointment with the private doctor six months before, were all still a bit confused as to the symptoms that I was showing and what they meant. So they arranged for me to set up a future appointment with a specialist when I returned to London.

My mum and my stepfather took me back down to stay at their place in the Berkshire countryside for the weekend to recover and everything seemed to settle down. I went back to London at the start of the week with no plan other than to keep my fingers crossed, take my meds and hope it wouldn't happen again.

I've realised that the scariest part of being ill is not knowing why or what it is, having to live in limbo feeling completely helpless and out of touch with your own body, unable to take control of your health. This experience has helped me to empathise with other people going through similar journeys.

Halfway through that week I started to feel similar symptoms coming on as before and my stomach once again started to bloat. After a phone call with my mum we decided it was better to be safe and both went straight away to the A&E department at Guys and St Thomas's Hospital in Westminster which overlooks the Houses of Parliament. Little did I know then that this hospital and that view would become a regular part of my life for the next two years.

I had a painful 24-hour wait in a holding ward in the hospital while my tests were analysed, and they tried to decide what was wrong with me. Then out of nowhere the following day a senior surgeon and a couple of doctors appeared. The surgeon was already dressed in his blue gown and I remember he had a very calm but strong and forthright demeanour, as he sat on my bed and said, "We need to perform emergency surgery on you, but don't worry, whatever it is we will get it out and make you better." His name was Dr Emin Carapeti and I'll always be truly grateful for the care he showed me, along with his surgical skill and experience in this field, which enabled him to successfully carry out the promise he gave to a very scared young man that day. He would be my surgeon over the next two years and four total operations.

Healthy for Men *front cover photographed in December 2005 and one month later after my first operation in January 2006, with colostomy bag.*

During the first operation they removed the blocked and damaged part of my colon and gave me something called an ileostomy. They bring part of the small intestine out through the abdominal wall which you then need to attach a disposable bag over, to catch your waste.

Waking up from the operation and seeing this was one of the most surreal experiences of my life.

Due to the aggressive damage that the disease had caused in my large intestine, they were starting to revaluate the original diagnoses of ulcerative colitis and now Crohn's disease and even cancer were on the table as potential causes, and I had to wait an agonising couple of days until the results of my biopsy came back.

I remember the day I was told that I had ulcerative colitis, not Crohn's disease or bowel cancer, the best of the bunch. I was sat next to my hospital bed post-surgery, watching the TV when a doctor came in and gave me the good news. As he left my bedside and walked out of the ward, I pulled the TV down in front to hide my face while floods of tears streamed out of my eyes. Later on I found out that at that moment, my mother, who was in London on her way into the hospital to visit me, had felt a sudden sense of relief and a weight lifted from her shoulders.

My case was written up in a medical journal, so I guess I have a slight claim to fame that my damaged colon is famous in medical circles.

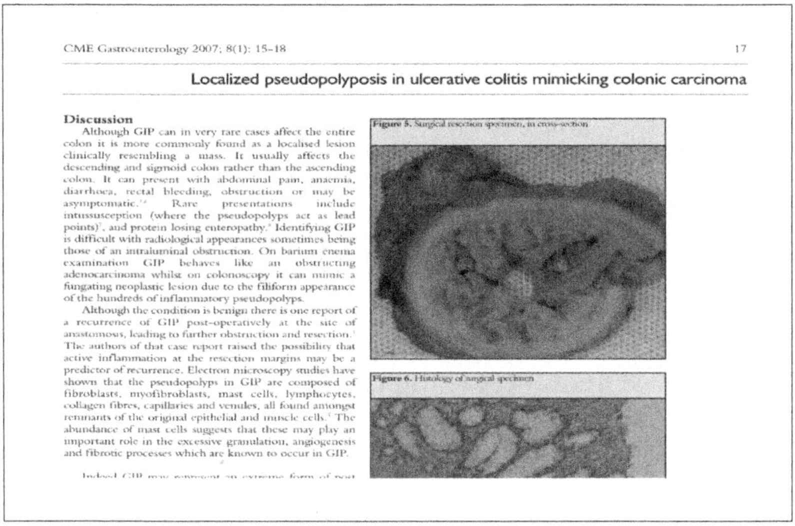
CME Gastroenterology 2007; 8(1): 15–18 17

Localized pseudopolyposis in ulcerative colitis mimicking colonic carcinoma

Discussion

Although GIP can in very rare cases affect the entire colon it is more commonly found as a localised lesion clinically resembling a mass. It usually affects the descending and sigmoid colon rather than the ascending colon. It can present with abdominal pain, anaemia, diarrhoea, rectal bleeding, obstruction or may be asymptomatic.[1-4] Rare presentations include intussusception (where the pseudopolyps act as lead points)[7], and protein losing enteropathy.[8] Identifying GIP is difficult with radiological appearances sometimes being those of an intraluminal obstruction. On barium enema examination GIP behaves like an obstructing adenocarcinoma whilst on colonoscopy it can mimic a fungating neoplastic lesion due to the filiform appearance of the hundreds of inflammatory pseudopolyps.

Although the condition is benign there is one report of a recurrence of GIP post-operatively at the site of anastomosis, leading to further obstruction and resection.[1] The authors of that case report raised the possibility that active inflammation at the resection margins may be a predictor of recurrence. Electron microscopy studies have shown that the pseudopolyps in GIP are composed of fibroblasts, myofibroblasts, mast cells, lymphocytes, collagen fibres, capillaries and venules, all found amongst remnants of the original epithelial and muscle cells.[5] The abundance of mast cells suggests that these may play an important role in the excessive granulation, angiogenesis and fibrotic processes which are known to occur in GIP.

Figure 5. Surgical resection specimen, in cross-section

Figure 6. Histology of surgical specimen

I left hospital after about seven to ten days – I can't remember now, all the visits blur into one – sporting a colostomy bag stuck to my left side where part of my small intestine was now coming out to catch my waste. I wouldn't be going to the toilet traditionally for the next 18 months.

I was also lucky to have a couple of bonding and life-changing moments with family in hospital, which I'll never forget.

Firstly, one with my brother which turned out to be an especially important and life-changing moment. I was having a 'woe is me' moment (to be expected really), commenting that I wouldn't be modelling again, that was it and I'd have to now give it all up, when my brother replied, "Don't let it control you Ad, you control it!" and it was at that moment my mindset shifted and gave me the strength to not only cope with that moment in my life but many others since.

The second bonding moment came with my father, who after his divorce with my mother when I was 12 had felt less and less like an important and integral part of my life. Due to the kind of surgery I had I was given epidurals to block the pain from my waist up to the bottom of my chest. These failed epically on two occasions when the catheter (tube) came out of my spine and over the course of 30 minutes my pain went from 0–10, too fast for the nurses to get someone who could sign off and administer morphine. It was on one of these occasions my father was visiting and luckily by my bedside squeezing my hand. I think he felt he was getting in the way so he asked, "Do you want me to leave?" to which I resoundingly replied, "No, I need you!" From conversations we have had since, that moment gave him back the feeling that his son needed him in his life. It was worth the pain just to give him that.

There is something very special and unifying when a family member goes through a health crisis. It really brings people together, transcending individual differences and situations, highlighting what and who is important in life. That's why people say that they wouldn't change a thing after going through a traumatic life experience; the experience itself is painful and one to forget, but it's what it teaches us about ourselves and life that is so precious and invaluable as we move forward with our journeys.

I was back in the gym six weeks post-operation, building my strength back up very slowly, having lost lots of weight and all the muscle I had proudly displayed only one month earlier when shooting the *Healthy for Men* magazine cover. I had never felt so weak and it was a real shock to the system to now find myself having to start all over again, but with the help of the *Rocky* soundtrack and a bit of 'Eye of the Tiger', I focused on Progress not Perfection, a mantra that I now use throughout my life and this book.

Building muscle only to lose it all again each time I went in for surgery, taught me a lot about my body and the many evolutions and transformations that we go through in life. You don't just do it once, it's a continuous journey, as is life. I've taken my body on many physical transformations, which has given me a great deal of awareness and understanding of the process, dedication and determination needed.

Later that year, in October 2006, I had the biggest of my operations. This time it was planned as opposed to an emergency, and was for the removal of my large intestine. It had been too badly damaged by the colitis to save and leaving it in would have put me at a greater risk of colon cancer in later years. During the same operation, they performed a procedure to create what is called an 'internal pouch', to function as a replacement for my colon. They bring down your small intestine and loop it back on itself to create a holding area, so that your body has more time to absorb water and nutrients, rather than it just leaving the body, a very similar function to a large intestine (colon). I like to affectionately refer to it as my 'bionic bowel'.

The operation becomes more complicated in people with longer torsos. My surgeon told me that the same operation on a 5ft lady had taken him one hour to perform as opposed to the 5 hours mine took (I'm 5ft 11). This is due to all the nerves and blood vessels attached to the small intestine that need to be carefully brought down with it and the longer distance in someone taller.

The recovery process was a long and brutal one with many very difficult moments throughout. After that big operation my white blood cell count went up and Dr Carapeti was concerned that I may have had a secondary infection, so that night I was taken back down to theatre and opened up again. This made it much harder for my staples to take and wound to heal.

My healing was further challenged because I could not keep down any food and needed a feed tube to be inserted through my nose, into my throat and down into my stomach, as my bowels were still 'asleep' (a common problem after digestive surgery). During this procedure you can imagine the gag reflex I was having as they inserted the tube, and where do you tense most when you're gagging on something? Your stomach muscles. You can imagine this is pretty painful after they've been cut in half, twice within 48 hours.

When I returned to my bed in the ward I decided to take a quick look at my scar and to my horror there was blood everywhere, not dissimilar to a horror movie. In a panic I got the nurse over to which she replied, "Oh don't worry, this always happens." I was shocked but also welcomed her calm nonsensical response, it was just the top layer of staples that had come loose and opened up, not the lower layer of stitching. Nothing too serious (for those outside my body) but this now gaping wound needed to be filled and dressed on a regular basis even after leaving hospital and it definitely prolonged my recovery.

It has left me with an impressive scar the length of my abdominals, but once again I recovered fully. I got back into the gym and back into modelling before I had my final operation in March 2007 to fully reconnect me and plumb my digestive system and 'bionic bowel' back in again. At the ripe old age of 29 I had to relearn how to use the toilet again and regain control of the muscles we take for granted that hold everything in for us.

At the time of writing this it is 15 years since the whole episode began. I've turned 42 and my health couldn't be better, although I wish I had known then what I know now about the damage that stress can cause, the healing properties of a plant-based diet and the body's ability to heal itself, if given the right conditions.

The first thing I would have done was switch to a plant-based diet, meditate and reduce all the chronic stress in my life as much as possible, both physically and mentally. I would have also used natural supplements and plant medicines such as herbs, essential oils and psychedelics to heal me on all levels, mentally, physically and spiritually. Hindsight is a wonderful thing and I can totally relate to what people say when they go through a traumatic experience and the invaluable lessons it teaches you.

It was horrific and scary at the time but looking back I wouldn't change it, because the lessons I learned and the inner strength it gave me were profound.

Modern medicine is great for emergency care and putting a 'band aid on a bullet wound' but from my experience useless at preventing the inevitable because it focuses on the symptoms and not the root causes. I really do hope this will change in the future, we need to look at and treat the individual, rather than just the disease.

No one ever asked me if I was stressed, worried, unhappy, or if I was sleeping well and what I was currently eating, they just sent me away with a different pharmaceutical every time. It's not the GP's fault either, it's the system we have created around health care and the profits that are made out of illness.

I will always be eternally grateful though for my skilled surgeon Dr Emin Carapeti, the wonderful nurses at Guys and St Thomas's Hospital in London, my family and friends, especially my mother who looked after me with so much love through some very dark days.

I believe everything we need to heal is in nature, we just need to reconnect with it, in every aspect of our lives, working with it, rather than against it and trust me, you are stronger than you think.

This same problem that we experience with personal health and healing on a symptom level is also the same problem that we experience on a collective level as human beings on this planet. We must take responsibility for the health of ourselves and the planet, and we must delve deeper to find the root causes of the challenges we face.

CHAPTER RECIPE

SCRAMBLED TOFU AND MASHED AVOCADO ON SOURDOUGH TOAST

This is the best tofu scramble I've ever made but then you'd hope that I'd only put the best in my book, right? It's the dark miso, paprika and turmeric that make it super tasty.

Tofu is without a doubt one of the blandest foods out there but is a really great blank canvas, because when you mix it with lots of herbs and spices, it takes on those flavours and provides awesome texture and nutrition to dishes.

You could eat the tofu on its own but adding it on top of some mashed avocado and sourdough toast gives you a filling and hearty plant-powered breakfast, packed full of flavours and textures.

Servings: 2–3 servings, depending on appetites

Ingredients:

Tofu Scramble

- 200 g firm tofu
- 5 big organic tomatoes
- 1 handful of spinach
- 1 onion
- 1 fresh clove of garlic
- 1 tbsp coconut oil
- 1 tbsp dark miso paste
- 1 tbsp yeast flakes (with added B12 is my favourite)

- 1 tsp paprika
- ½ tsp turmeric
- Salt and black pepper (good quality flaked sea salt or Himalayan salt)

Mashed Avocado on Sourdough

- 1 avocado
- 1 tbsp apple cider vinegar
- 1 tbsp extra virgin olive oil
- 1 tbsp yeast flakes
- Salt and black pepper
- Sourdough toast

You will need:

- 1 large frying pan
- 1 spatula
- 1 large bowl (for breaking up tofu)
- 1 small bowl (for mashing avocado)
- 1 chopping board
- 1 sharp knife
- 1 fork for mashing
- 1 tablespoon for measuring and serving
- 1 teaspoon for measuring

Cooking Method:

1. Sauté a chopped onion and a clove of garlic in a little coconut oil and hot water. I like using hot water to help sauté as it softens the veg quickly without burning the veg.
2. Then add 5 big tomatoes chopped into small cubes and a tablespoon of dark miso and leave to simmer, adding a little more water to keep it loose in the pan

and to create a bit of sauce.

3. Then in a large bowl crumble a 200g block of organic non-GMO tofu and add 1 tsp paprika, ½ tsp turmeric, pinch of Himalayan salt and pepper, mix thoroughly and then add to the pan, with a big handful of spinach and put the lid on to heat through. The tofu will soak up all the lovely juices in the pan.
4. Add 1 tbsp of yeast flakes to the mixture just before serving.
5. Then mash up some avocado in a small bowl with salt, pepper, 1 tbsp apple cider vinegar, 1 tbsp of organic olive oil and 1 tbsp yeast flakes and spread on top of some toasted sourdough.
6. Top with the tofu scramble mixture, then marvel at how damn tasty a dish you've just made from plants!

Top Tip: Top with sprouts and seeds for extra texture and nutrient density.

CHAPTER 2

TIME FOR A CAREER CHANGE

"We must be willing to let go of the life we've planned, so as to live the life that is waiting for us."
Joseph Campbell

There's nothing quite like realising the fragility of your own existence in terms of a career based solely on the way you look externally and how quickly that can all change and be taken away from you. My experience with illness and surgery helped me to realise that it would be much healthier for me to find a new career based on a set of skills rather than looks alone. After all, six packs do indeed come and go but you only get one large intestine (at the time of writing).

Finding my Inner Geek

Between 2007 and 2009 I was lucky enough to work on the model recruitment team for the Abercrombie & Fitch clothing store in London. This meant that while recruiting good looking guys and girls to work in the store, we could go to our own modelling castings etc. and have time off for modelling jobs. It was the perfect job and scenario at the time to support the ups and downs of my modelling career and I worked in a great team of guys and girls, who I became good friends with.

One day while out recruiting I was having a phone conversation with my brother, who would once again be a catalyst for positive change in my life.

We were having a heated brotherly discussion about a computer problem I was having. Bear in mind my brother was and still is a massive computer geek, who has earnt fantastic money from contracting as a software engineer for some big companies.

He pointed out to me during this conversation in a very brotherly and not so understanding way, that what he was telling me was easy to understand and that I should really know what he was saying. As you can imagine, this conversation didn't end on a high. I came off the phone and began to curse him at first, which then turned into a feeling of admiration that he had found something in his life that he truly loved, live and breathed – he had found his 'inner geek' and I knew that I needed to find mine.

It didn't take long for this train of thought to uncover what I had known for years but had been reluctant and afraid to explore. What was it that I would love to talk and learn about 24/7 and not get bored of?

It was the gym, training, lifting weights, nutrition, supplements and everything that went along with the fitness lifestyle. I had finally realised my own 'inner geek' and that was it, I knew I needed to become a personal trainer.

I was also lucky enough to have befriended a great personal trainer at the gym in Oxford Street where I trained, Dan

Boulle. He became a good friend and offered me lots of advice for getting started in the industry. Dan had a great balanced perspective on training and a wealth of knowledge about human anatomy, he was a great mentor and role model for me, showing me how a professional personal trainer should operate. Dan was the first of three mentors that I would have through my career and went on to open his own premium training facility in central London for elite performance athletes and clients.

So, within days I had found a course that allowed you to split payments over 18 months. The course was a blend of distance learning and online course work, with one Saturday classroom session per week, which I couldn't wait to be part of. It made me realise how easy learning can be when you love the subject being taught. For the first time in my life I became the class geek, putting my hand up to answer questions at every opportunity.

I had a bit of an advantage over many on the course who were new to training and fitness in that I had read and learnt so much about training through my own personal study and body transformation experiences, through both modelling and illness over the previous ten years.

I was also very lucky with the Abercrombie recruitment team job that I was still doing during the week. If we hit our targets and got our hires each week then managers generally left us alone during the day to wander the streets of London. Although we spent many hours skiving off in coffee shops, I used this time to sneak off to internet cafes and complete my personal training course work online. Sometimes you do what you must, to realise your goals.

Another Body Transformation

As I was embarking on my study to become a personal trainer and getting ready to leave my modelling days behind, I realised that I also needed to find a new challenge or way of staying in great shape.

When you're modelling you have the added incentive of staying in pretty good year-round shape because you never know when opportunity may knock for an underwear or fitness job. It keeps you focused and now I wanted to see just how far I could push my body, especially two years post-surgery. I wanted to prove to myself that I could not only still achieve the kind of body that had got me onto a magazine cover but that I could make it even better than before.

So, I decided to enter my first fitness modelling show at FAME UK August 2009 in Brighton. I would enter the Bodybuilding category as well just for the laugh and experience, plus the Male Fitness Model category which was the category that my body was more suited to, due to its size and shape.

I put myself through a hermit-like existence for three months leading up to the show, which most first timers do, eating a diet that had very little nutrient diversity and was very strict. I pretty much ate oats, egg whites, chicken, broccoli, rice and whey protein shakes for three months and although I was more shredded than I'd ever been, in the week leading up to the show my gums started bleeding due to a lack of nutrients. It was a sign that if I was going to do this again I needed to be a little smarter with my nutrition.

Looking back, it was also a stark realisation that even those eating meat and animal products can be deficient in nutrients, when eating a bland and badly planned diet. It was well planned from a calorie perspective but not from a nutrient dense perspective.

So, from then on, each time I entered a show my goal was always to not only improve how I looked from the last show but also to streamline the process, making it less stressful, more efficient and more nutrient-diverse than the one before.

The first show was a shamble of organisation, which I came to realise accompanies most amateur bodybuilding shows. It was also a baking hot day in Brighton and everyone backstage was so dehydrated, with fake tan running everywhere, but I had a lot of fun that day.

I came 3rd which was a great reward after all the training and especially after the years of illness and surgery. The whole process had taught me once again what it takes to transform your body, Consistency and Commitment.

I then took part in a show each year in 2009, 2010 and 2011, coming 3rd again in the Male Fitness Model category in 2011, but the competition was getting much harder. The fitness show world was exploding in popularity thanks to social media and there were more guys entering, in better and better shape.

FAME UK 2009, 2010 and 2011

I'd also now been a personal trainer for a couple of years in London, moving from Fitness First in South Kensington to their flag ship 'Black Label' gym in Baker Street, where I had been surrounded by some very knowledgeable and successful trainers. I used the environment to improve my knowledge base by asking questions and absorbing as much information as I could from them.

I went on several courses around this time and was very lucky to have a fantastic mentor in Dave Petersen. He was my manager at Baker Street, who I had followed from the first gym in South Kensington. When he was promoted to new manager of Baker Street he asked me if I wanted to move with him, so I jumped at the opportunity. We regularly had geeky chats about training and nutrition; his enthusiasm after so many years in the industry was infectious and from what I gather is still to this day.

I have a lot to thank Dave for. He helped instil in me his

enthusiasm and work ethic in the early days. Having a great mentor is so important, and I had been blessed to have met two great role models who helped get my career on track, especially in an industry that is known for its 'cowboys'.

Time to Leave London

Towards the end of 2011 I was feeling quite claustrophobic in London and needed a change of scenery and an adventure. I was very lucky that my girlfriend at the time was turning 30 and we had been gifted a two-month trip to South East Asia for her birthday, so we packed up from London and off we went, with a view to maybe moving abroad.

We managed to cram an amazing amount of destinations and travelling into those two months, visiting Beijing, Xian, Shanghai, Hong Kong, Philippines, Borneo, Kuala Lumpur, Singapore, Deli, Goa, Mumbai and Dubai on the way home.

We were lucky enough to visit the orangutan orphanage in Borneo and witness the tragedy that is unfolding with deforestation due to the palm oil trade. When you fly into Borneo you can see for miles around the monoculture of palm trees grown to satisfy the world's hunger for palm oil. It's only now as a vegan and more conscious consumer that I can join the dots together.

During the trip, my nan who was 89 at the time had a fall, damaged her hip and was admitted to an old people's home, so on returning to the UK I decided that I wanted to be closer to her and my father in Devon. We decided to move nearby to Torquay and try our luck there.

I thought that I was committing career suicide at the time, leaving London as a personal trainer and moving to Devon. I didn't believe I'd find somewhere worthy enough to match where I had been in London; but I was very wrong, it was the best career move I could have made.

In January 2012 I was lucky enough to find an amazing local, privately owned gym group called Winners 2000, who had three gyms in the local area, Torquay, Paignton and Newton Abbot. I fitted right into the Newton Abbot gym which was at the time their best and biggest gym. Built in an old bowling alley, it has a 30-metre indoor track, outdoor gym and outdoor circuit area. It was a heavenly gym for a personal trainer to train clients in, so much space and natural light, when compared to many of the stuffy basement gyms in central London.

In December that year at the National Fitness Awards – an award federation for privately owned fitness businesses – we won National Gym of the Year 2012, which was a huge achievement. It felt incredible to have left London behind and to land right in the lap of such a great organisation and to be an integral part of the winning team that year, with more success to come in 2013.

In 2013 I also decided it was time to enter another couple of fitness model shows, the WBFF Denmark show in April and then the WBFF London show in November. I didn't place at either one, even though I was in my best shape having improved at each event, the standard and number of guys entering these shows had increased ten-fold in just the last year and the London show would be my last one.

WBFF Denmark 2013
and my final show WBFF London 2013

When I arrived at Winners 2000 in 2012 I'd been requested to write a personal trainer development programme by Simon Jeffery the owner and my new and third mentor. He became my new 'training geek' outlet and he was instrumental in boosting my own professional confidence through the continued support he gave me. The development programme for trainers was one of the elements in the case for us winning gym of the year in 2012 but would also prove to be key in the award that I won in 2013.

When Simon first suggested that I run for Gym Based Personal Trainer of the Year 2013 at the National Fitness Awards, I cringed at the thought, but thanks to his support, encouragement and persuasion I put my case file together and entered the competition.

In December 2013, just one month after competing at the WBFF London fitness model show, I went up to Manchester for the National Fitness Awards with the rest of the team from Winners 2000 and was awarded Gym Based Personal Trainer of the Year 2013. It was an incredible moment in my professional career to be recognised for my work and knowledge, one that I will never forget and it made that conversation I had with my brother just four years previous to that, even more significant. Thanks to Simon and the support of the team at Winners 2000, I had found, unleashed and had my inner geek recognised.

I've been very lucky to have had three great mentors throughout my career, they really are worth their weight in gold, and I have much to thank them for.

Winning Gym Based Personal Trainer of the Year 2013 at the National Fitness Awards in Manchester.

CHAPTER RECIPE

MEXICAN BLACK BEAN CHILLI WITH CUCUMBER RAITA

Basically, rice and beans spiced up, the cornerstone of any nutritious vegan diet – when combined, grains and beans contain all the essential amino acids, along with plenty of fibre, and there's no cheaper and nutrient dense meal you can make.

It's such a delicious and easy-to-make combination and one of the first that I started making and eating when I first went plant based. It provides the right blend of protein and carbohydrates (with little fat), perfect for a post-workout feast, and can be easily cooked in bulk and eaten fresh, at home or on the go.

Feel free to add more cayenne if you need more spice. The cucumber raita is the perfect accompaniment to cool down any hot dish, be it made with Mexican, Thai or Indian spices.

Servings: 2

Ingredients:

- 225g organic fresh chopped tomatoes
- 230g cooked, drained and rinsed black beans
- 125g wild, brown or white basmati rice
- 100g organic tinned sweetcorn
- 1 red pepper sliced
- 1 white onion sliced
- 1 little gem lettuce sliced

- 1 fresh lime
- 1 handful of fresh coriander chopped (save a few leaves to garnish)
- 1 vegetables stock cube or 1 tbsp of dark miso
- 1 tsp smoked paprika
- 1 tbsp of avocado or coconut oil
- 1 garlic clove chopped
- ½ tsp cayenne pepper

You will need:

- 1 medium saucepan to make the chilli
- 1 large saucepan to cook the rice
- 1 sieve to drain the beans and rinse
- 1 chopping board
- 1 sharp knife

Cooking Method:

1. Add the rice to a pan and cook as per instructions on the packet. Wild or brown rice are great but do take much longer; white basmati is much quicker for the timings of this dish.
2. Heat up a pan on a medium heat with the avocado or coconut oil and add the sliced onion and red pepper. Add 100 ml of water and put the lid onto the pan and allow them to soften and go translucent.
3. Add the chopped tomatoes, paprika, cayenne pepper, garlic, stock cube, juice of half the lime and the coriander and turn onto a low heat, allowing it to simmer and develop all the flavours. Be wary of adding any more salt due to the stock cube, wait until the end to taste.
4. Once the rice is cooked, add the black beans and

sweetcorn to the chilli and heat through for a minute. Line a bowl with the chopped lettuce, serve the rice in the middle with the chilli and a couple of generous dollops of the cucumber raita. Squeeze the rest of the lime over the dish and garnish with some coriander leaves.

CUCUMBER RAITA

A delicious little accompaniment for any spicy dish. Use a nice dollop to serve and refrigerate what you don't use.

Servings: 4–6

Ingredients:

- 150g of organic cucumber grated coarsely
- 150g of coconut or non-dairy plain yoghurt
- 2 sprigs of fresh mint leaves finely chopped
- ½ fresh lemon juice
- Pinch salt

You will need:

- 1 grater
- 1 mixing bowl
- 1 chopping board
- 1 sharp knife

Cooking Method:

1. Grate the cucumber coarsely into a bowl and get rid of the excess water.
2. Add the rest of the ingredients into the bowl and mix well.
3. Add a pinch of salt to taste, just before serving.

CHAPTER 3

THE VEVOLUTION IS COMING!

"It's not what we know that gets us into trouble, but what we know for sure that just ain't so."
Mark Twain

The two years in Devon had been incredibly fruitful for me from a career perspective – I'd worked for a great organisation with wonderful people – and also from a family perspective. I'd spent much time reconnecting with my nan and my dad; living so close to them had been amazing for our relationship, which I'm so grateful for. But I was single again and really missing my London crew of friends, along with the buzz and opportunity that being in a big city brings. I decided that I needed to move back to London in January 2014.

It was a tough decision for me to make, especially after Simon and Winners 2000 had been so supportive of me for those two years and instrumental in the success that I'd had while I was there. I had built some great friendships with colleagues and I didn't want it to look like I had used them in winning this award and was then running away back to London with it. But I just wasn't happy living there anymore and needed a fresh start and a new challenge. I guess that's what can happen once you've realised and achieved a big goal – there's a need to move on to the next.

Everyone was incredibly supportive of my move though, including Simon, all my colleagues, clients and members at the gym. Simon said many times before I left that I'd always be considered one of the family at Winners 2000 and there would always be a job once I got bored of London again. Thanks Si.

At the time I moved back to London in February 2014 I was also nursing the start of an annoying shoulder injury (shoulder bursitis) that I had picked up through my training during the last contest prep a couple of months before. Unbeknown to me at the time, this shoulder injury would take most of 2014 to recover from and would be the catalyst for the biggest shift in my consciousness during my life so far.

Had I not picked up the injury then I would have most probably carried on training with the bodybuilder mindset and eating the heavy animal-protein-based diet that I had done for the past few years.

Protein Prison

Having the injury made me re-evaluate the way in which I was training. I could no longer train with the high volume, body-part specific approach that most bodybuilders do, at least not while I had this injury, so I was forced to adopt a more functional, fun and relaxed approach to my training with less structure, lots of patience with regular physio and rehab exercises.

At the same time, due to the change in my training goals and methods, I realised that there was less of a need to consume the six meals a day I had been accustomed to eating for so long as part of the bodybuilder training. At the same time the need for so much protein reduced, which had the knock-on effect of making me question just how long in my life I intended to keep up this search for muscle and the body beautiful, surrounded by the protein prison I had erected around my eating habits. This type of lifestyle was starting to feel less sustainable the more deeply I thought about it.

This more mindful approach to food and life in general was also given momentum after a dinner party that I had with three new London friends. The topic of the night surrounded consciousness, life force, the universe, etc. It was one of those nights where you leave full of energy and a whole new set of questions for life to answer.

I look back on this night now as a defining moment and the start of my spiritual awakening.

Mindful Eating

I never intended to or even considered the thought of becoming vegan, although when I look back, something was starting to unravel inside my subconscious, and I was becoming more open to a new path and perspective.

I decided that I would eat less meat and the meat that I did consume would come from more ethical and humane sources. I've since come to realise that these terms are relied upon by those looking to reinforce their own meat-eating habits. We are all always looking for evidence to back up our habits; it gives us comfort and helps us to avoid having to shine a light on them, because when we really see these habits for what they are, we must go through the painful process of breaking them down and changing long-held belief systems.

CHAPTER RECIPE

ITALIAN PASTA AND BEANS WITH CASHEW PARMESAN

This is another simple, tasty and delicious recipe to get your head around, that I've been making on some of my workshops for a while now. So it's tried and tested, perfect for beginners and anyone who loves Italian flavours.

This is also a great post-workout meal that is high in protein and carbohydrates and low in fat if eaten without the cashew parmesan. If you want additional texture, cheesy flavours and a few more calories then add some of the cashew parmesan on top before serving – it takes it to another level.

Again, this recipe and can be easily cooked and eaten fresh, at home or on the go.

Servings: 2

Ingredients:

- 230g cooked, drained and rinsed cannellini beans
- 225g organic baby plum or pomodorino tomatoes cut in half
- 200g gluten-free pasta (100g per person)
- 100g spinach
- ½ aubergine, chopped into small cubes
- 1 garlic clove finely chopped
- 1 handful of fresh basil torn (save a few leaves to garnish)
- 1 tbsp of avocado or coconut oil

- 1 tbsp extra virgin olive oil
- 1 tbsp of balsamic vinegar
- 1 vegetable stock cube
- Salt and pepper

You will need:

- 1 medium saucepan to make the sauce
- 1 large saucepan to cook the pasta
- 1 colander or sieve to drain the pasta and rinse the beans
- 1 chopping board
- 1 sharp knife

Cooking Method:

1. Bring a pan of water to the boil with a pinch of salt.
2. Heat up a frying pan on a medium heat with the avocado or coconut oil and add the finely chopped garlic and cubed aubergine, and sauté for a couple of minutes until the aubergine softens.
3. Now add the chopped tomatoes, fresh basil, crush and sprinkle the vegetable stock cube and the balsamic vinegar, leave to simmer on a low heat, adding pepper. Taste before adding more salt as the vegetable stock cube will have seasoned the sauce enough.
4. While the sauce is simmering, add the pasta to the boiling water and simmer until cooked al dente.
5. Now add the cannellini beans and spinach to the sauce and stir through, wilting the spinach and heating the beans through. This only needs a couple of minutes to avoid the beans breaking up through overcooking. If the sauce looks a bit too thick then add a little water to loosen it up.

6. Once the pasta is cooked, drain and add the pasta to the sauce along with the extra virgin olive oil and stir through. Serve topped with the cashew parmesan and garnished with a few basil leaves.

CASHEW PARMESAN

This will become a staple topping for all your Italian and maybe many of your other plant-based dishes. It really tastes incredible and takes seconds to make, literally!

Servings: N/A

Ingredients:

- big handful of organic cashews
- handful of yeast flakes (preferably with added B12)
- big pinch of salt (I like Himalayan or flaked sea salt)

You will need:

- 1 food processor, blender or grinder

Cooking Method:

1. Add all the ingredients to a food processor, blender or spice grinder and blend until you have a fine dried parmesan look and feel.

CHAPTER 4

EMBRACING THE PLANTS

"People eat meat and think they will become as strong as an ox, forgetting that the ox eats grass."
Pino Caruso

In September 2014, a few months after the dinner party that set my plant-powered wheels in motion, I was invited to another dinner party, this time specifically a vegan and raw food one, by a friend who I knew was a great cook. I was excited to see what we'd be eating and I was not let down by the raw courgetti with Italian sauce, the raw vegan lasagne and the raw chocolate cake for dessert.

The food literally blew my mind. I didn't know that it was possible to create such amazing vegan dishes let alone raw ones. This had such a positive impact on my transition because I remember thinking that night, if I could eat like that every night, I wouldn't miss meat at all.

That night I also met someone who would prove instrumental in my future development and link to the plant-based movement in London. I met Damien Clarkson an activist and long-term vegan, we enjoyed some great discussions that night on the ethics of plant-based nutrition, opening my mind up further to this new lifestyle. It was another nudge in the right direction for me.

A couple of years later, Damien and his now wife Judy went onto launch the leading plant-based festival Vevolution, which I have met many of my plant-based contacts and friends through. I have also since spoken at Vevolution on several occasions. It was those presentations that were the catalyst for me to start writing my story, that grew into this book. It never ceases to amaze me how life twists and turns, with chance meetings along the way with awesome people that can lead to magical new beginnings.

Meat and Two Veg

Part of the problem with people transitioning to a plant-based diet is that they are unaware of the infinite possibilities you can create with a diverse range of plants.

Rather than being the limiting dietary approach that everyone thinks it will be, a wholefood plant-based diet (WFPBD) can be extremely expansive and creative.

In the UK especially, we are brought up on the 'meat and two veg' approach to meals with a big slab of meat being the central focus to all our meals and a few overcooked vegetables as an afterthought.

So, the mere thought of losing the meat and being left with just the boring two vegetables is not the most appealing one, but in fact you remove the meat and it becomes nutritionally essential that you replace it with a whole host of other plant foods, giving you a much more nutritionally diverse meal than you had before.

It just requires you to step out of your comfort zone and explore.

Spiritual Diet

Later that month I was booked on a spiritual retreat in the UK to help with my own personal development. In preparation for this retreat I had to follow a strict vegan diet for two to three weeks prior to the event, which would help to cleanse my body, remove impurities and allow a much deeper spiritual connection to myself.

So, this was a perfect time to actually try out a full vegan wholefood plant-based diet. If anything, it was a great opportunity for me to put myself in the shoes of a potential client who might come to me living a plant-based lifestyle, so that I could see things from their perspective and deliver nutritional advice through experience rather than ignorance.

After the retreat I felt surprisingly well and had enjoyed the increased freedom that living plant based had given me. For the first time in my adult life I had managed to start letting go of the need for animal protein in every meal and released from my 'animal protein prison'.

So I decided to go pescatarian for a month to experiment further and monitor how I felt just eating fish and dairy; then I decided the next step was to phase that into a vegetarian diet. This actually didn't feel that healthy to me as I started to become more reliant on dairy, which I'd never eaten a huge amount of, as I had never considered it to be a healthy choice long term, even when I ate lots of meat.

All the while my subconscious was nudging me gradually towards a vegan diet but I was quite happy exploring new food choices rather than becoming obsessed with any label that I might have been becoming.

Then two weeks into my vegetarian phase I decided to watch three documentaries over the course of ten days that would change my life.

At the time I had a more heightened level of consciousness thanks to the deeper spiritual work I had been doing, along with the more mindful, questioning approach to my food choices. I was ready to open my eyes, ears and heart and make any changes necessary to make sure I was aligning with myself and my surroundings.

The following documentaries that I watched had been recommended to me by friends and it all started to unravel.

Firstly, I began with ***Cowspiracy*** which tackled the argument against meat eating from an environmental point of view and was very in-depth, and well researched with good science and hard-hitting statistics behind it. I'd never considered the environmental factors before I watched *Cowspiracy*; it was a refreshing new perspective and it added more fuel to my growing plant-powered fire.

A few days later, I watched **Gary Yourofsky's** YouTube seminar called **'The Best Speech You Will Ever Hear',** one of the most compelling and passionate people I've heard talk about the reasons why not to eat meat. During some of the footage in his presentation things started to shift for me.

I suddenly found myself in floods of tears as I realised that I had been a willing participant in an industry causing so much trauma and suffering.

I was now on a roll and wanted to learn more. I was fully open and ready to take onboard the truth, so 24 hours later I watched ***Earthlings***, which put the proverbial nail in my meat-eating coffin. If you can watch that documentary to the end and don't feel the need to at least rethink your animal-eating habits, then you need to check your heart is still beating and relearn the meaning of empathy and compassion.

VEGAN MYTH BUSTING
VEGANS ARE SO PUSHY

I know we are pushy sometimes because I felt it before I went vegan; and that second documentary I watched had been sitting in my YouTube 'Watch Later' list for 18 months before I decided to watch it, mainly because it had been 'pushed' onto me by a very exuberant vegan a friend Anthony Lowther, which made me resistant to the content and his message.

Lesson to vegans everywhere – no one ever turns vegan because they've been forced into it, and in fact no one ever changes their mind about an argument if someone is standing in your face telling you that you're wrong and a bad person for living the life and making the choices you have been.

But now I am on the other side of the fence and have

been part of the community on and offline since 2014, I understand the reasons why vegans can come across so pushy sometimes, and there's three of them:

1. **Empathy** – You have a new deep sense of empathy, the ability to share another being's feelings or experiences by imagining what it would be like to be in their situation and it hurts you.
2. **Compassion** – You have a new deep sense of compassion, a connection to the sadness for the suffering of all non-human life and it hurts you.
3. **Frustration** – You've finally joined the dots, seen the light and it all makes sense. The two above feelings are also so strong that it's frustrating as hell that not everyone can see what is glaringly obvious to you now*.

*Not dissimilar to the actions of 'born again' Christians or ex-smokers!

But it is only now that it has become obvious to you. We must all remember (unless you've been a lifelong vegan from birth) that we too have made many unconscious decisions about eating animal products and therefore must recognise that everyone is on their individual point in this journey as well, as we once were.

Who am I to judge someone when back in 2013 I shook my head in annoyance at vegan clients as I rammed the paleo diet down everyone's throats and ate steak for breakfast, which were my nutritional beliefs at the time.

It's so important that we adopt a non-judgemental, encouraging, supportive and science-based informative approach, for people to base their decisions on, rather than a religious ideological approach that is forced onto others.

Be the Change

The trouble with becoming more aware in so many areas of life, but particularly regarding our food chain, is that you can no longer live your life with your head in the sand. This means that current affairs, atrocities and the infinite number of wrongdoings going on in the world affect you.

At the time I was going through my transition I was also having this overwhelming feeling of 'How the hell am I, one person, supposed to make a difference to the world?!' then it all suddenly made sense to me after hearing Gandhi's famous saying:

"Be the change that you wish to see in the world."
The tattoo I had in 2015

It had such a profound effect on me that I had it tattooed on my forearm, to remind me that change, big or small, always starts with one person, one thought, one mind and one action. If that thought or action is profound enough that other people recognise the benefits of making that change, they too will adopt that behaviour and so it begins and grows like wildfire.

Our external world will never change, unless we all take responsibility for our own inner worlds and change them first.

It dawned on me that we make three to six food choices a day (especially in the fitness and bodybuilding worlds) – that's over a thousand food-based decisions that we all make every year. When you expand that to 1 million or 1 billion people you can start to see what a huge impact our food choices can have, the collective power that we all possess, just by changing what we decided to put on our plates and into our mouths every day.

Taste Buds and Trauma

There are many facts about the meat industry that we are all aware of even as obliging meat eaters. We know animals are born and bred to be killed for our plate and palate, and although we know it goes on we don't really want to accept and face the reality of it and certainly not let it penetrate deep into our hearts. We know once it's there, resistance is futile and we have to acknowledge it from our most natural innate characteristics of compassion, empathy and love, and this means you have to make serious changes to your life.

Change is challenging and an important factor to acknowledge when looking at the difficulty people have in transitioning from one long-held nutritional habit to another is that for many people food is used as a comforting tool in times of stress. And there are many everyday stresses and pressures to deal with, such as work, career, finances, family, relationships, emotions, etc., so it's no wonder that the last thing people are willing to change is the eating habits that have provided them with some form of comfort through challenging times. Thus the decision to let that go feels like a huge one to make.

People who knew me and knew that I had a love for nutrition and nutritional science just assumed that I had made the shift to a plant-based diet purely for my own nutritional reasons; it couldn't be further from the truth.

At the time I was seeing so much conflicting evidence and research from both sides of the argument (I still am), and as someone who is aware of the way bias can be given to any number of studies thus drawing a conclusion to suit the argument, I decided to not let any of these arguments cloud my decision. As there were truths on both sides, I needed something more certain.

The one fact that I knew in my heart to be true, that didn't need to rely on research papers and hearsay, was the fact that other living beings were being bred, fed and slaughtered in prison-camp-like conditions just so we could enjoy eating them. With such indisputable evidence to back my decision I was able to make the change without looking back.

I found my strong WHY and it has carried me forward ever since. Having a strong why makes it easy being in restaurants when there's nothing on the menu that interests you, because you're not putting your taste buds first anymore.

Once you fully accept and acknowledge the link between your taste buds and the trauma that is being inflicted to satisfy them, then the transition to a vegan plant-based diet becomes much easier and more straightforward.

In the Beginning

A couple of months into my transition in January 2015 I had lost about 4 kg in weight. There was lots of flu going around which I had managed to avoid, even after working six day weeks for two months, but when I picked up a severe cold that month and was ill on and off for about three weeks, friends and family started to worry. Because I was now a vegan, that became everyone's suspicion as to why I was experiencing some ill health, rather than the fact that it was the 'flu season' and everyone else was also ill at that time of year, many of whom were eating diets that contained animal products.

Looking back at photos from my brother's wedding at the end of January 2015, I wasn't looking my best but while I passionately fought off these negative arguments with family and friends I couldn't help but have slight doubts in the back of my mind as to whether this way of life would work for me, especially after having been through so much with regards my health and digestive system. I was moving into unknown territory, but I had faith and a strong emotional why as my anchor.

At my brother's wedding in January 2015, 4 kg lighter

At this point I decided to take some pressure off myself and added a few eggs and some dairy back into my diet for a couple of weeks, as I felt at the time my body needed a boost of calories and I needed to stop trying to be the 'perfect vegan' straight away. I would embrace the process of change, allowing my body and mind to adapt at a slower pace to the nutritional changes and the lifestyle pressures that it brings.

I eventually got rid of the cold I had experienced, and my immune system became stronger, I regained all the weight I had lost in a couple of months and began growing in the gym once again.

I also did the 10,000 Kettlebell Swing Challenge, which took me about six weeks to complete and as my shoulder injury had now cleared up I started working on regaining the strength I had lost with my squat, dead lift and bench press.

In the months that followed I also fine-tuned my diet back to a pure plant-based vegan diet. I dropped the eggs and only ate a vegetarian option if I was out with friends and there was no other choice, which I then progressed away from completely.

This personal experience though did highlight the dichotomy that we face between our morals choices and our bodies requirements, I think ultimately we all have to find a solution that improves our health whilst reducing the trauma and suffering it leaves behind and having awareness of the impact that those choices make on the world around us, only you can make the choice, consciously.

Immune and Strength Boost Needed

During this time when I was trying to boost my immune system and my strength back in the gym, I did a couple of things that really helped:

1. **Fresh ginger, lemon juice and cayenne pepper shots** – These fiery little shots really help to alleviate any mucous on the throat, reduce inflammation and boost the immune system. I still drink them during the winter months now if I feel a cold or flu coming on and I swear by them.

To make them just juice, mix and store in the fridge, drinking shots as and when you need them throughout the day:

- 600 g fresh ginger
- 3 lemons
- Add 1 tsp cayenne pepper

Ginger, lemon and cayenne shots

I also now sometimes add equal amounts of carrots to ginger for additional antioxidants, beta carotene (the precursor to vitamin A) and its skin healing and anti-cancer benefits. The additional sweeter carrot juice also takes the fiery edge off the ginger if you want a more pleasurable drinking experience.

2. **Creatine monohydrate**
   This had a huge impact on me regaining the strength and power in the gym that I had lost since going vegan. We are unable to obtain creatine from natural plant food sources, so it must be synthesised to make it vegan certified. Creatine is formed in the human body and thus also in animal protein; it is used for energy production, specifically for muscular strength, speed and power.

You can take the synthesised version of creatine in a white powder or boost your body's natural production of creatine by supplementing with spirulina, the blue green algae that you can buy in powder form.

Spirulina contains the three main amino acids that the body requires to synthesise creatine naturally, these are:

- Glycine
- Arginine
- Methionine

Due to my lack of a large intestine it is also quite easy for me to lose water, so I have found that supplementing regularly with creatine helps my body to maintain good water balance, maintaining fullness in my muscles.

Progress Not Perfection

One of the biggest lessons that I've learnt throughout this process and something you will hear me talk about throughout this book and at any of the events I speak at, is that those wanting to transition away from consuming animal products to the vegan lifestyle should focus on Progress not Perfection.

We live in a society that likes to class things as black or white, right or wrong, good or bad, all or nothing, and we seem to have trouble grasping the concept that sometimes it's better to do just a little, rather than nothing at all. Maybe we do this because it makes our lives easier when it comes to classifying situations, people, objects, opportunities and lifestyle choices.

If you speak to many 'new age' vegans, they'll most likely shy away from the 'vegan' label due to the negative connotations that it has attracted, and favour the current trendy, inoffensive and more flexible term of 'plant based'.

I branded myself The Plant Powered PT rather than The Vegan PT for a couple of reasons:

Firstly, to avoid scaring off potential clients who might land on the scale anywhere from 'occasional meat eater' to 'ready to go all in', who might think that I would bring hellfire and damnation down on them if they even spoke of free-range eggs or looked longingly at a ball of mozzarella.

Secondly, I wanted to make this a more inclusive way of living, with less judgement, offering those who wanted to know more but didn't know where to start, a safe place to enquire, without scrutiny.

After all, I was a huge meat eater, so who am I to judge where people are with their ethical and moral standpoint on consuming animal products. We must never forget where we have come from, it helps us to understand and educate others more effectively.

I'm very proud to be part of this plant-powered, plant-based, vegan movement, because I believe it's the easiest way we can all bring about huge amounts of positive change to the world we live in, reducing suffering and trauma, while improving our individual health and the environment in the process.

By adopting these plant-based eating habits and using the

1,000-plus meal choices we make each year, we can all really make a difference.

So, it is not in my interest to alienate people who may be thinking of going just meat-free Monday or vegan from Monday to Friday, as it is always going to be better for someone to eat less meat two days a week rather than not bothering at all.

Once you start this journey and experience the benefits of a diverse plant-based diet, you naturally want to keep experiencing more of the benefits as it resonates more deeply with you, so you try it a little bit more, maybe an extra day, maybe a whole week, maybe even a month.

My more inclusive and flexible approach may upset some of the more hardcore vegans out there, but I'm not bothered. I don't care what they think, they are already vegan, they have already made the positive change to their life which I applaud, and so they are not the people I am trying to reach out to and help.

None of us are perfect, even vegans. We all die, even vegans no matter how much kale we eat, but we can all support each other in progressing towards a better more inclusive world, with less judgement, by focusing on Progress not Perfection.

CHAPTER RECIPE

PERFECT POST-WORKOUT SMOOTHIE

This is the ultimate post-workout smoothie, high in protein, medium carbohydrates, and low in fats.

It contains carbohydrates from the bananas, maca to help bring the body back into hormonal balance, antioxidants from the raspberries, iron and zinc from the pumpkin seeds, vitamin C from the baobab which will help with iron absorption, and electrolytes from the coconut water and bananas to replenish lost minerals.

You could also add a handful of spinach or kale to this to increase the nutrient density, levels of antioxidants, anti-inflammatory effects and alkalising of the body which is beneficial post-workout. But a word of warning – it will turn your nice pink smoothie more of a brown colour, but it's worth it for the nutrients, not so good for an Instagram photo!

Servings: 2

Ingredients:

- 100 g raspberries
- 50 g pumpkin seeds
- 2 bananas
- 2 scoops of vanilla or plain plant protein powder
- 2 tsp of baobab and maca
- 600 ml of coconut water
- 6 ice cubes

You will need:

- 1 blender

Cooking Method:

1. Add the ice cubes and coconut water first to the blender then the rest of the ingredients on top, so that they don't stick to the blender jug.
2. Blend on full power for 20 seconds and serve.

CHAPTER 5
COMBINING PASSION WITH PURPOSE

"Be yourself, everyone else
is already taken."
Oscar Wilde

That dinner party I attended a year before in April 2014 had set me off on a journey of self-discovery and plant-powered enlightenment I could never have imagined. Even in just a year I had done much inner work on myself, contemplating not only life and the human condition but also how I could make a difference in the world.

I had been a personal trainer for six years at this point, and I just couldn't at the time see a way in which I could combine this new-found conscious way of living and looking at the world, while being stuck in the fitness industry, which was resonating less and less with me at the time.

Time for an Adventure

I hadn't been on a travelling adventure since the end of 2011 and having gone through many personal shifts over the past year I felt I needed to detach from my life, to get some space and clarity as to where I was going with all this new knowledge.

It was now June 2015 and I had been on several spiritual retreats in the UK over the last year, watched many documentaries and listened to many podcasts on increasing my consciousness. There was one topic that kept coming up for me to explore, which was the visionary plant medicine called 'ayahuasca'. Traditionally from the Amazon, it is a combination of hallucinogenic plants that are brewed into a thick brown liquid or 'tea' (which gets worse every time you drink it) and is consumed during a ceremonial practice with a small group and a Shaman to direct the ceremony.

This psychedelic drink has been taken for thousands of years by the indigenous people of the Amazon. It helps give them insights, a deeper connection to their lives, to mother nature, the planet and the ability to heal on physical, mental and spiritual levels. We in the Western world have completely disregarded these in terms of the holistic approach to healing, choosing to focus purely on the physical symptoms with pharmaceutical man-made chemicals; an approach to healing that from my own first-hand experience was not an effective long-term treatment of chronic disease and the reasons behind it.

This really sung to me on many levels and I knew it was something I was eager to explore; going to the Amazon and taking part in a week-long ayahuasca retreat would give me an adventure both externally and internally.

I later learned that 'She', 'Mother Ayahuasca' or 'The Madre' (all terms that refer to the feminine mothering spirit of the plant medicine) calls you when it is time for you to become more awakened and to drink the 'medicine'.

There was one retreat that kept popping up in podcasts and documentaries I had watched called Blue Morpho Tours based in the Peruvian Amazon jungle. They had great reviews and were obviously highly regarded in this field of psychic exploration, so I decided to book with them for the following January 2016.

On a cautionary note, it is incredibly important that you perform your due diligence when deciding to partake in an ayahuasca ceremony. Before you travel down to the Amazon jungle and book on a retreat, do your homework first before paying your money. It is not to be taken lightly, this is serious and powerful work. It should not be treated like a social drug-taking experience. It is a very strong and serious plant medicine and teacher that forces you to do lots of deep spiritual 'work' on yourself; some of these lessons can be very hard, upsetting and challenging to work through but profoundly healing at the same time. You need expert helpers, guides and those who are immersed in the Shamanic Arts of Plant Medicines, to make sure that your journey is a safe, expansive and rewarding one.

It will however be one of the most incredible and life-changing experiences of your life, if you're willing to let go and look beneath the 'veil of life'.

While I was booking my ayahuasca retreat with Blue Morpho Tours, I had also heard of another healer called 'John of God' in Abadiania Brazil, a now 75-year-old man who had the ability to heal others and channel spiritual entities since he was a teenager. For many years he had been giving up Wednesday to Friday every week to help heal others at a 'spiritual hospital' called 'The Casa de Dom Inacio'.

(Unfortunately, in December 2019 Joao de Deus, or John of God, received a prison sentence following a multiple rape and sex abuse allegations, although at the time of writing this 'The Casa de Dom Inacio' is still active helping and healing people. It's so sad that people in a privileged position are corrupted so frequently by the power they wield; my thoughts go out to those affected by his actions.)

Every day there are about 300 people who turn up to patiently wait in line to see him and to have 'spiritual surgery' performed on them to help heal many ailments. Many people have gone there with terminal illnesses and left cured.

I had been told that it was a crazy place, with strong energy and it all sounded tantalising and crazy enough to spark my adventurous spirit and warrant a visit as part of my trip. So I decided to book plane tickets after my ayahuasca retreat and check it out.

Then two of my best friends mentioned to me that they wanted to do the trek to Machu Picchu in Peru and wanted to visit South America at the end of 2015 as well, so not wanting to miss out on this adventure I decided to get involved in that as well and do the five-day trek before heading down to the Amazon for the ayahuasca retreat.

I had managed to manifest an adventure of epic proportions with three different parts:

1. First with two of my best friends James and Ash, I would visit the longest mountain range in the world, the Andes, visiting Cusco and onto the Salkantay Trek to Machu Picchu, one of the hardest and highest routes (15,000ft) to the 'Lost City of the Incas'. We would then visit Huaraz, a city with beautiful views of the snow-capped Cordillera Blanca mountain range, before returning to Lima, the capital of Peru for a few days of sightseeing, great vegan food, paragliding and surfing lessons.

Victorious on the last day of our five-day trek, the view overlooking Machu Picchu at the top of Huayna Picchu

2. I would then leave my buddies and head off to Iquitos in southern Peru, the jumping-off point into the Peruvian Amazon jungle, a city whose only access is by air or boat. I would then join my group with Blue Morpho Tours and go off into the jungle for my seven-day ayahuasca retreat.

Receiving my cup of ayahuasca on the last ceremony at Blue Morpho Tours in the Amazon jungle, from the Shaman Maestro Don Alberto

3. To complete the trip, I would then fly to Abadiania in Brazil, from Lima, and via Sao Paolo, to visit John of God and the Casa de Dom Inacio, to see what all the fuss was about.

The entrance to Casa de Dom Inacio and the view from the healing gardens, where I sat and meditated many times

At the time I wondered how on earth I was going to afford such an epic trip, but I knew I had to do it and I knew I had to do all three parts. I wouldn't think about the money,

I would just make it happen, which I did.

It has been one of the best examples in my life of 'being in the flow', connecting with a purpose that was so important and authentic to my journey that work, clients and money just flowed into my life for the next six months, enabling me to pay for the whole trip.

It wasn't until two weeks before I left that I was lying in bed one night thinking about the trip ahead, that I realised that this was no chilled beach holiday that I had booked myself onto. I knew deep inside that this was going to be an incredible yet challenging adventure I was about to undertake and I wasn't wrong; the whole trip was a real coming of age journey for me and each part tested me differently in ways that I could never have imagined. Once I returned I felt like I'd been on a 'spiritual special forces' course.

I could write a small book just on the adventures and challenges I faced and went through in those five weeks, but there were three very distinctive moments of the adventure that stood out that challenged me and pushed me beyond my comfort zone.

In the 24 hours before our trek to Machu Picchu I started suffering from altitude sickness or a stomach bug. I was vomiting and had diarrhoea on the mountain during the first day of our trek, thousands of feet above sea level amongst snow-covered peaks. I struggled and struggled and as the day went on felt more like a 90-year-old man than a 30-year-old. At the end of day one I collapsed in my tent and it was touch and go if I was going to make day two; but I did thanks to some plain food, an antibiotic and on the morning of day two a coca tea with sugar – a brew very popular in higher altitude regions due to its ability to alleviate symptoms of altitude sickness. It is made with the leaves of the coca plant that contains alkaloids, which when extracted chemically are the source for cocaine base. This could explain my renewed enthusiasm for life that day!

I then experienced ayahuasca ceremonies that pushed me close to the edge of what I could take mentally and physically, violently purging on many occasions (vomiting into a bucket during ceremonies, which removes physical, emotional and spiritual toxins from the body); and other ceremonies that left me laughing hysterically for hours, both having profound and long-lasting effects on my psyche, leaving me in a state of wonder every night among the sounds of the jungle and a deep feeling of gratitude for my life and all within it.

I then had a week of solitude at John of God, forced to be in my own head and deal with all the thoughts and emotions that would come up. I experienced 'spiritual surgery' and then mediated for three hours in the 'current room' (a room where 30-plus people sit and meditate to generate love and energy for the healing work which is performed), sitting on a wooden bench unable to move for three hours with only my own thoughts and inner demons to work through. Then on the final day of my trip, having been through so much over the five weeks, I lay on a crystal healing bed for the last time (a bed that you lie on under a series of different coloured crystals and lights relating to your energy chakras) and had this deep epiphany moment where I felt, for the first time in my life, that I was now a man with the power and energy that I was ready to commit to something much bigger than my individual self – either a mission, a relationship or a family.

As you can imagine, these experiences and this whole adventure had a very deep and profound effect on me and it has played a pivotal role in my life over the past few years. In both my personal and professional life, these experiences continue to do so, and probably will for the rest of my life.

Rebranding my Business

After having such an incredible adventure, full of experiences that have left an indelible mark on me for the rest of my life, everything started falling into place.

A couple of months after coming home I finally realised how I could leverage my years of experience in the fitness world along with my passion for plant-based nutrition and making a difference to the planet.

THE PLANT POWERED PT
TRANSFORM YOUR BODY AND OUR PLANET

I decided to go all in and rebrand my personal training business from Cover Fitness to The Plant Powered PT with the tag line 'Transform Your Body and Our Planet'. I knew veganism was on the rise but that I was an early adopter in terms of the fitness industry. It was a market that was a couple of years off maturing in terms of building a vegan client base for personal training, as most people in the industry were still promoting a heavy animal-protein diet. I knew I would be alienating myself from some potential clients but I believed that my time would come and I wouldn't be happy unless I was being totally authentic and true to myself, in every element of my life.

CHAPTER RECIPE

OVERNIGHT BIRCHER OATS

This recipe is so simple and easy to make, it just needs a little bit of pre-planning the night before so that it's ready for breakfast and you can eat it at home or on the go.

Servings: 1

Ingredients:

- 300 ml nut milk
- 100 g oats
- 1 apple grated
- 1 handful of walnuts
- 1 handful of blueberries
- 1 tsp of cinnamon
- 1 scoop of plant protein powder (whichever is your favourite)
- 2 dried dates chopped
- 2 dried figs chopped

You will need:

- 1 grater
- 1 container to soak the oats in
- 1 bowl to serve or 1 container to transport the oats if you're on the go

Cooking Method:

1. The night before, add the oats, nut milk, cinnamon and grated apple together in a sealable container, mixing together thoroughly before putting in the fridge.

2. If you want to increase the protein content of the meal just add a scoop of plant protein powder, whichever flavour takes your fancy, and mix in thoroughly.
3. Serve topped with the blueberries, walnuts, dates and figs.

CHAPTER 6

WHAT I EAT IN A DAY

Dear Animals, sorry it took me so long.

A cacophony of delicious and colourful dishes that range from green smoothies, mashed avocado on toast, burrito bowls, bean burgers, black bean pasta, jack fruit ragu, tofu scramble, vegan mac and cheese, vegan lasagne, vegan cottage pie, all kinds of warm and cold salads, tofish chips and mushy peas, mushroom steaks, frozen fruit ice cream, energy balls and cashew parmesan, many of which you will experience through the recipes in this book.

Mashed avocado on rye toast, black bean pasta and vegan mac 'n' cheese

VEGAN MYTH BUSTING – BEING VEGAN SOUNDS COMPLICATED AND LIMITING

I think this vegan myth stems from our own rigid belief systems and food programming from an early age, someone takes away the meat and we are lost to know what to replace it with. Doesn't that sound crazy? But that's how accustomed we have become to having meat so readily available wherever we go and how polarised we have become when looking at a plate of food.

Complicated – What's complicated about eating as many different coloured plant-based foods that you can find (fruits, vegetables, beans, nuts and seeds)? By focusing on a diverse range of colours you will ensure that you're consuming a nutrient-dense diet, as opposed to a very calorie-dense diet made up of meat and dairy.

I think the 'complicated' label comes from the way the media have portrayed potential deficiencies, and that you need to plan a vegan diet more carefully than any other diet to avoid them, which is of course untrue. It may at first seem complicated to someone who has lived a life that has revolved around meat, but only because it's not a way of living they are accustomed to; it's actually very simple once you let the meat and dairy go.

Just like doing anything that you've never done before, it requires a certain amount of learning in the beginning, there are a new set of skills and perspectives that you must learn.

Limiting – Many of us were brought up on the 'meat and two veg' mindset (which sounds very limiting to me these days). The 'two veg' being an afterthought with so much focus on meat as the central player in most meals. Whereas with a vegan diet you're not locked into that central food group anymore, which leaves you more room to be creative, think outside the box and explore the multitude of different coloured plants that are available to us, which in turn makes cooking fun, exciting, challenging, delicious and above all nutritious!

Remember you don't need to go vegan 100% overnight and give yourself a label. Lean into the process, take your time, read, learn, acquire these new skills, explore and enjoy a whole new life that is waiting beyond a door that has been blocked by a massive steak for years.

CHAPTER RECIPE

THAI GREEN VEGETABLE CURRY WITH CAULIFLOWER RICE

This dish is ideal to make if you want to have a higher fat and low carbohydrate meal, as it supplements the traditional rice for cauliflower rice, which soaks up all the juices.

This is one of my staple favourites when I'm on a low carbohydrate day or phase of eating. I love Thai food and this is a nutritious dish that's simple and tasty.

This could also be eaten fresh or taken with you on the go.

If you can't find edamame beans or would like a higher protein version then you could supplement them for baked tofu – tofu cut into small cubes, marinated in tamari, 1 tsp of sesame oil and baked on foil in an oven for 10–15 minutes. A very simple and delicious way of consuming tofu.

Servings: 2

Ingredients:

Vegetable Stock

- 200 ml of water
- 1 tbsp of dark miso
- ½ finely chopped nori sheet or dried sea vegetable

Main Dish

- 200 g coconut cream (from the top of a tin of coconut milk)

- 150 g broccoli
- 150 g edamame beans fresh or frozen
- 30 g chopped cashew nuts
- 60 g Thai green curry paste
- 4 baby corns sliced in half
- 4 spring onions
- 1 sweet pointed red pepper chopped
- 1 handful of shredded Thai basil leaves
- 1 thumb-sized piece of ginger finely sliced into match sticks
- 1 clove garlic chopped
- 1 tbsp of avocado or coconut oil
- 1 tbsp sesame oil
- ½ fresh lime juice

Cauliflower Rice

- 1 cauliflower
- 1 tbsp of avocado or coconut oil
- 1 pinch of salt

You will need:

- 1 large saucepan
- 1 measuring jug
- 1 chopping board
- 1 sharp knife
- 1 food processor
- 1 large frying pan

Cooking Method:

1. Start making the cauliflower rice first as it can be allowed to cook slowly and left as the curry is cooking. First take off the leaves and stalk and cut into pieces.

Then add to a food processor and pulse it until it's a rice-like texture.

2. Put in 1 tbsp of oil into a large hot pan and put in the rice, then add a pinch of salt and gently fry for 5 minutes, keep stirring so that most of the water evaporates, and the rice starts to brown slightly. Having a large frying pan will allow the water to evaporate much easier.
3. While the cauliflower rice is cooking, pour 200 ml of boiling water into a measuring jug with the dark miso and the finely chopped nori sheet and put to one side for the stock.
4. Heat up a pan over a medium heat with the coconut cream, allow to come to the boil and then add the curry paste, ginger, garlic and mix for a few seconds to let the aromas release.
5. Pour in the stock and bring back to the boil then add the spring onions, baby corn, broccoli, sweet red pepper and edamame. Cook through for 5–10 minutes.
6. Then stir through the Thai basil and half the lime juice before serving.
7. Serve the cauliflower rice with the curry, top with sesame oil, chopped cashews, a few Thai basil leaves and a squeeze of lime.

CHAPTER 7
REPLACING MEAT

"The idea that some lives matter less is the root of all that is wrong with the world."
Paul Farmer

I understand what it's like. I ate meat for the first 36 years of my life and certainly from my 19th year my consumption must have doubled each year as I passionately pursued the body beautiful and became further entrenched into the 'more meat equals better' mindset of the fitness and bodybuilding world at the time.

Eating steak, lamb or any other cuts of meat for breakfast was also the norm for me. I absolutely loved a rib-eye steak, sharing a chateaubriand, a homemade burger, trips to Nandos for a half chicken, spicy rice and coleslaw. So, you would think that for me to let go of eating meat must've been like a drug addict going 'cold turkey' (excuse the pun).

It's not just the meat you're letting go of, but you're changing the social dynamics and bonding between friends and family over food. They remain with their old habits as you decide to change yours, choosing life and the reduction of trauma and suffering over taste and tradition.

I remember fondly one of my last meat feasts, a bonding

meal for two with my stepfather. We shared a huge rib of beef at the restaurant Hawksmoor in London and finished it off with a nice Canadian bourbon.

Have I missed meat?

Funnily enough, not really, which really surprised me considering the amount I used to eat, although I craved smoke salmon for a little while after going vegan. I mean, I still love the smell of a barbecue – no one ever gave up meat because it didn't taste good – but I chose to prioritise the life of an innocent animal over my need to satisfy the taste buds.

Vegan Doesn't Automatically Mean Healthy

You can technically be vegan these days, and still be unhealthy, due to the rise in vegan junk food and meat alternative products. You only need to visit some vegan festivals and look around to see that vegan does not necessarily mean looking healthy.

Anything that's covered in batter and deep fried in vegetable oil, is not going to be good for your health long term, whether that's a piece of chicken, fish, tofu or a Mars bar!

Likewise, you could eat meat a few times per week alongside a dense plant-based diet and be healthy. This book is about showing you that there is an alternative that is just as good, if not better for your health and certainly better for the environment and those animals we share it with.

It is exciting though as a vegan to go to an event where you can eat and enjoy all the foods on offer without having to read labels or enquire about the source of ingredients. It's a relief to have access to traditional foods like burgers, pizzas and cupcakes that are all free from animal products.

But I think the community needs to be cautionary about this as we move forward. Are we jumping out of the frying pan and into the fire?

If we want to get technical about the optimal vegan diet then we are talking about a wholefood plant-based diet (WFPB) which is the healthiest way to eat vegan. There's nothing wrong with enjoying occasional 'junk food' but it shouldn't be seen as an everyday staple in your diet.

Food technology is having a huge impact thanks to increased demand, along with many prominent vegans on social media, bringing out cookbooks and experimenting with plant foods to create meat replacements.

I have been served vegan 'meatballs' at a vegan restaurant before and I had to go and ask the chef to actually confirm if they were really vegan and not meat – they tasted spectacular and had me fooled. There are many new amazing plant-based start-up food companies popping up all over the world who are creating some groundbreaking meat replacement products, such as Impossible Foods who have created the plant-based 'Impossible Burger' available across the US in Burger King. There is also Beyond Meat, who created the 'Beyond Burger' available in many food outlets across the UK now. It has a slight bloody excretion made from plant-based iron. Both are becoming a global sensation and are leading the way for plant-based food innovation which was reflected when Beyond Meat floated on the US stock exchange, over doubling their valuation in a day.

There are some genuinely awesome products out there to satisfy anyone's taste buds and to alleviate the fear of missing out, while transitioning to a new plant-powered diet.

Aside from all these new products there are staple plant-based foods that provide us with a source of high protein, meaty textures and different flavours.

High-Protein Plant Foods

Most of the protein obtained on a plant-based diet comes from legumes, grains, nuts and seeds but there are a couple of high protein sources that make a great high protein meat replacement addition to the diet, but just like everything else that you eat, rotate it as often as possible with other protein sources, to prevent reliance and increase nutrient diversity.

1. **Tempeh** is one of my favourites and one of the most beneficial plant protein sources. It is made with soybeans that are fermented into a cake, giving it the nutritional edge over many other sources. The earliest known reference to tempeh was in 1815 and is a staple protein source in Indonesian cuisine.
2. **Tofu** making was first recorded during the Chinese Han dynasty some 2,000 years ago. It is also called 'bean curd', which is a fresh, cheese-like product made by curding soy milk. Tofu is bland on its own but very versatile as its texture lends itself to all kinds of cuisines, absorbing the flavours of any dish.

3. **Seitan** is made using wheat gluten, the protein portion of wheat that gives bread dough its elastic quality. It is generally mixed with lots of herbs and spices. It has been used as a meat substitute for centuries in China and Japan, where it was developed by vegetarian Buddhist monks. This goes great in burgers, stews, stir fries, kebabs, etc.

All the above draw some opposing views from purest vegans who argue about soy products linked to estrogenic elevation and other disorders but as you can see they have been used for centuries in oriental cuisine. The problem these days lies more in the sources of soybeans which have been genetically modified, and/or sprayed with pesticides rather than the soy itself.

VEGAN MYTH BUSTING
SOY WILL AFFECT MY HORMONES!

Not so fast, firstly we need to look at these two types of estrogen:

- Phytoestrogen
- Mammalian Estrogen

These two are regularly confused and are not the same, but easy for mainstream media to bundle together, which then muddies the water.

A **Phytoestrogen** is a plant-derived xenoestrogen not generated within the endocrine system but consumed by eating phytoestrogenicplants. Its name comes from the

Greek *phyto* ('plant') and estrogen. Estrogen created and found in the body is the hormone which gives fertility to female mammals, also known as **Mammalian Estrogen**.

There are many foods that contain phytoestrogens and if you're going to throw soy out because of this then you'd also have to throw linseed (flax), sesame seeds, wheat berries, fenugreek, oats, barley, beans, lentils, yams, rice, alfalfa, mung beans, apples, carrots, pomegranates, wheat germ, rice bran, coffee, liquorice root, mint, ginseng, hops, bourbon whiskey, beer and fennel.

There has been much scaremongering regarding soy and its effect on estrogen levels in males and females, increasing the risk of hormone-related illness etc. but far from it, they may actually have the opposite effect.

Plant estrogens do not eliminate all of estrogen's effects, but may help to minimise them, maybe even reducing breast cancer risk and menstrual symptoms. For men and boys, the phytoestrogens in soy may not appear to have an effect on hormone levels and have not been shown to affect sexual development or fertility. In fact some research studies show that men consuming soy have less prostate cancer and better prostate cancer survival. However, I must say that much of the evidence seems to be conflicting and inconclusive.

But I would always look for organic non-GMO varieties of tempeh and tofu where possible, thus reducing any other issues to do with the farming of them. Or you can make your own, as you can with seitan at home. I would also try and find an organic wheat gluten to make your seitan with.

Just like any other food group, if you do have a genuine intolerance to soy, like wheat, gluten, dairy, etc, then just don't eat it and if you do then as my granddad once said to me...

"Everything in Moderation, Including Moderation!"

Cooking with Tempeh, Seitan and Tofu

All of them can be used very creatively in high protein plant-based meals and the different texture of each one lends itself to different dishes. Here are a few examples of how to use them:

- **Tempeh** – Chopped finely or blended slightly in a food processor gives it the texture of mince, perfect for use in bolognaise or burgers.
- **Tofu** – Crumbled with hands or a fork makes it perfect for scrambled tofu or again as a mince like meat texture, or as a fish substitute for tofish and chips (see recipe at the end of this chapter). Tofu is very bland which makes it boring on its own but perfect when blended with lots of herbs and spices, as it will take on all the flavours in the dish.
- **Seitan** – Comes in a block much like a steak and can be sliced to use in stir fries, sandwiches or in stews. You can also make it at home with vital wheat gluten, which comes as a powder. Combine it with different herbs and spices, roll it into a dough, then steam or boil it to solidify into a meat-like texture, which can then be sliced, fried, grilled, etc. just like a steak or burger.

Plant-Powered Supergrains

These are alternative grains that make a nice change to the usual rice, and contain high levels of nutrients and amino acids (protein). They make for great additions to dishes such as salads and curries or as texture in nut roasts and burgers, these include:

- Quinoa
- Amaranth
- Buckwheat
- Spelt
- Barley
- Millet
- Bulgar Wheat

Plant Protein Powders

The three most widely used plant sources found in protein powders are generally hemp, pea and rice due to the range of essential amino acids found in them.

Usually a good protein powder will have a blend of two or all three of them to give the powder a broad amino acid profile, perfect for building muscle and recovery after strenuous training, but not always essential (see Vegan Myth Busting – Stop Worrying About Protein).

The Six Steps

I like to simplify training and nutrition as much as possible, and I wanted to create a simple template to help myself and others understand what constitutes a nutrient packed plant-based meal, so I came up with this simple six-step approach.

These steps ensure each meal contains a balanced profile of protein (amino acids), carbohydrates, fats and other essential nutrients, such as fibre, vitamins and minerals.

- **Don't eat today what you ate yesterday** – This ensures nutrient diversity and helps avoids deficiencies.
- **Choose a protein (25% of the plate)** – Beans, legumes, tofu, tempeh, seitan or plant protein powder.
- **Choose a carbohydrate (15% of the plate)** – Starchy root vegetables, grains and/or fruit.
- **Choose a fat (10% of the plate)** – Nuts, seeds, avocado, olives, oils (coconut oil and avocado oil to cook with and extra virgin olive oil, hemp and flax seed oil to add to dishes).
- **Choose different coloured vegetables (50% of your plate)** – The more colours the merrier.
- **Choose different combinations of herbs and spices** – This brings the whole dish together and makes any flavour possible.

Of course, plants are made up of synergistic combinations of nutrients, it's only humans that reduce food to the isolating labels of protein, fats and carbohydrates, so although I class seeds such as hemp and chia as fats, they do also contain good levels of protein. So you see you don't have to worry about it, it's everywhere!

The Six Steps are a very simple approach but by following them you will ensure that your diet is rich in nutrient diversity and density, as they say…

Diversity is the Spice of Life!

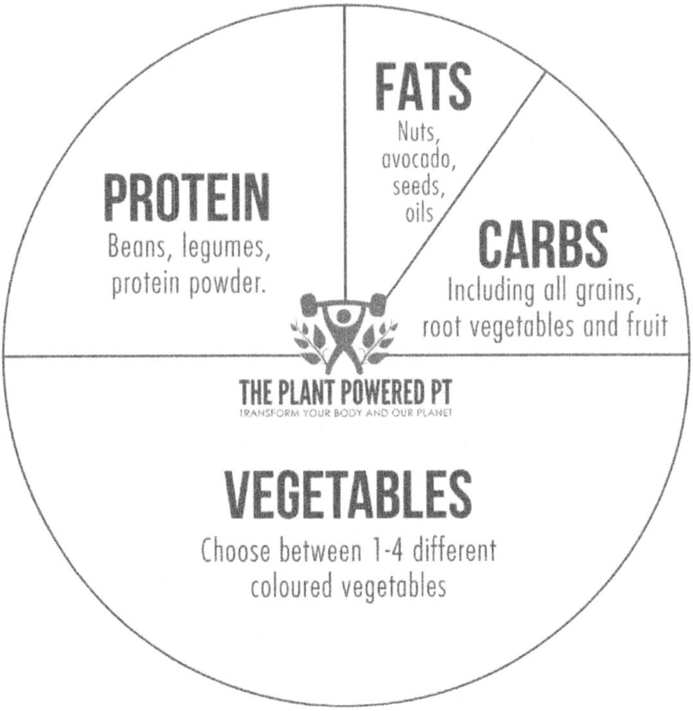

The plate diagram above is an easy-to-use visualisation of how this balanced plant-based meal could look.

CHAPTER RECIPE

TEMPEH KIDNEY BEAN BURGERS WITH A SIMPLE SALAD

This recipe utilises tempeh, a great plant-based source of protein, with a deep flavour and meaty texture, with kidney beans for a delicious and satisfying burger.

I'm really hit and miss when it comes to making burgers, but after much experimenting and trial and error, this recipe works well and has been tested by many people on some of my past workshops. It's a winner!

Just add a slice of vegan cheese towards the end of cooking the burgers and throw in a bun with some sliced tomatoes, lettuce leaves and some vegan siracha mayonnaise for a naughty treat.

Or enjoy as part of a super healthy meal with a big green simple salad instead like below.

Servings: 6–8 burgers depending on size

Ingredients:

- 1 pack of tempeh cut into small cubes
- 230 g kidney beans drained and rinsed well
- 100 g oyster mushrooms chopped
- 60 g gluten-free breadcrumbs
- 4 garlic cloves crushed or finely chopped
- 2 tbsp nutritional yeast
- 2 tbsp tamari or gluten-free soy sauce

- 2 tbsp avocado or coconut oil
- 2 tsp smoked paprika
- 2 tsp dried thyme
- 1 white onion halved and sliced
- Salt and pepper to season.

You will need:

- 1 large flat bottom frying pan
- 1 food processor
- 1 chopping board
- 1 sharp knife

Cooking Method:

1. Heat the avocado or coconut oil in a large frying pan over medium heat. Add the sliced white onion, thyme and oyster mushrooms. While they are softening for a minute, slice the tempeh then add to the pan and cook for about 3 minutes.
2. Then stir in the beans, garlic, and nutritional yeast. Cook for 2 more minutes. Stir in the tamari and smoked paprika. Remove from the heat to cool slightly.
3. Put the gluten-free bread into a food processor and blend until you have a bread crumb.
4. Add the tempeh/bean mixture to the food processor and blend on pulse until you have a coarse mixture. Taste and adjust seasoning with salt and black pepper.
5. Form the mixture into six patties, making sure they are not too thick, so they cook evenly. Cook the burgers in a lightly oiled flat pan over medium heat until golden and heated through, about 3 minutes per side.

SIMPLE SALAD

Sometimes all you need with a couple of tasty filling burgers is an equally fresh, tasty and nutritious salad to accompany the deep, meaty flavours of the tempeh.

The dressing doesn't have to be anything more than some good quality olive oil, fresh lemon or lime juice and some salt and pepper. Let the plants do the talking.

Servings: 6

Ingredients:

- 5 large tomatoes chopped
- 1 cucumber chopped
- 2 carrots grated
- 1 pack organic baby leaf spinach
- 1 pack organic rocket

- 1 romaine lettuce chopped
- 1 pack alfalfa, broccoli or other sprouts
- 1 tbsp shelled hemp seeds
- 1 tbsp chia seeds
- 1 tbsp pumpkin seeds

Dressing
- 4 tbsp of extra virgin olive oil
- 1 fresh lemon juice
- Salt and pepper

You will need:
- 1 large mixing/salad bowl

Cooking Method
1. In a large bowl mix the chopped lettuce, spinach, rocket, grated carrots and sprouts then scatter the chopped tomatoes and cucumber over the top. Sprinkle with hemp, chia and pumpkin seeds and then add the olive oil, lemon juice, salt and pepper and toss everything together before serving.

CHAPTER 8
LETTING GO OF DAIRY

"The greatest ethical test we're going to face is the treatment of those who are at our mercy."
Lyn White

I drank so much milk growing up, gallons of it. I loved the stuff, on cereal for breakfast, served at school for lunch and more than likely a glass or two in the evening with dinner and then a hot chocolate before bed. Looking back on my early years, my body fat levels suffered from the effects of dairy excess, until it mostly disappeared from my diet and the weight fell off.

One thing you realise when going fully plant based and letting go of dairy is that it's in everything – there's milk, powdered milk, powdered egg and cheese in so many products. Cheese is everywhere – cheese on cheese, cheese stuffed into pizza crusts – and everyone just laps it up, due to its addictive nature, especially when you combine saturated fats and simple carbohydrates, two of the leading causes of diet-related illness today.

Health

In my experience, getting rid of dairy out of the diet seems to cause the biggest problem for most people as opposed to the meat side of things. People find going vegetarian easier because they just substitute everything with cheese. This is one of the reasons why the vegetarian diet can be very unhealthy for many people.

As a personal trainer one of the most common goals clients come to me with is the wish to improve the ratio of body fat to lean muscle (body composition). Even when I was an avid meat eater the first thing I would get a client to do if this was their primary goal, would be to drop the dairy out of their diet, as it makes losing body fat so much harder. This is because many people have become intolerant to dairy and it can cause much inflammation in adults, making it harder for your body to lose excess fat, not to mention the growth hormones found in milk that could elevate the risk of certain cancers. After all, it's a liquid that is designed to grow baby cows into huge mammals, not humans.

Ethics

As one of my guiding principles of plant power is to 'Reduce Trauma and Suffering' I can't condone or consume dairy because of its ethical implications. Once you open your eyes you also realise that the dairy industry is just as bad as the meat industry, if not worse. Cows must be pregnant to produce milk, which is meant for their babies. Therefore to maintain regular production of milk to supply the demand, cows are artificially inseminated year-round, their babies removed from their sides after birth and once they are no longer fit for milk production are sent to the meat industry for slaughter.

Not to mention the plight of their offspring. Boys are either killed or sent to be part of the cruel veal industry, girls suffer the same fate as their mothers and are forced into a life of slavery and milk production.

All this for a food product that is not naturally meant for humans but for baby cows.

When you build a business around animal products your livelihood is based on the continued enslavement of those animals. In a capitalist society there must be continued growth, to achieve continued profit, which then leads to continued suffering as animals are reduced to mere production-line commodities.

How do we stop this? We stop creating businesses and economies based on profiting from animals and their by-products. If we carry on this madness we are no better than the machines from the film *The Matrix*, harvesting humans for their energy.

In the documentary *Cowspiracy*, Dr Michael Klaper makes a few valuable points:

"The purpose of cow's milk is to turn a 65lb calf into a 400lb cow as rapidly as possible." He goes on to say, "Cow's milk is baby calf growth fluid."

Doesn't that make you think about the potential health issues that could arise from drinking and eating products made from cow's milk.

Baby Calf Growth Fluid.

Luckily for us now the modern era has ushered in a whole new type of milk made from nuts and plants, you can buy them in the shops everywhere or make them easily at home. The fact is that we don't need to drink milk from animals anymore, you can get super tasty and creamy plant-based alternatives now everywhere – better for us, for the cows and the environment. Another win-win scenario.

Non-Dairy Options

There're so many options out there now, going dairy-free has never been easier and tastier.

Nut Milk

This couldn't be simpler to make. You can soak some almonds or cashews (or any nut you fancy) for a couple of hours or overnight. This helps to lower the phytic acid in the nuts which can act as an anti-nutrient that prevents the absorption of some essential minerals in the gut (although phytic acid also has beneficial properties in terms of reducing cardiovascular disease, cancer and diabetes). We don't need to really worry too much about this unless you have a mineral deficiency, so soak where possible but don't worry about it if you're unable to.

Then blend the soaked or un-soaked nuts with filtered water (as a ballpark figure I make about 1.5 litres of nut milk with about 150g of nuts), one date and a drop of vanilla extract or the seeds from one vanilla pod.

Then filter this through a nut milk bag or hessian sack to collect all the sediment, and there you have deliciously creamy, slightly sweet plant-based milk.

Cashew Cream

This stuff is seriously good. Picture the moment you have a dairy-free chocolate brownie fresh out of the oven, all warm and gooey inside but it just needs something creamy to complement the taste and textures. You think, 'If only I had something creamy to go with the brownie', then you realise you have some cashew nuts in the cupboard, so you chuck a handful or two in the blender along with a small bit of filtered water or nut milk and blend until creamy, adding more liquid depending on desired consistency. Hey presto, the creamiest and most simple non-dairy cream out there. If you have the time, then of course soaking the nuts beforehand as above is advisable but if not, it's not the end of the world.

This can easily be turned into cashew ice cream with a few tweaks (see end of chapter recipe)

Cashew Cookies

So, I stumbled upon this recipe myself after making my first ever batch of cashew milk and was blown away by it.

After you've drained the pulp from the nut milk, don't throw it away. Throw it in a bowl instead and add cacao nibs, goji berries, some agave, maple syrup or honey and cinnamon, mix it all together and spread out on some baking paper on a baking tray. Then bang it in the oven for approximately 45 minutes–1 hour on a low heat and keep checking until crispy. Then chop up some dark chocolate and sprinkle on top while the cookie is warm so it melts.

Vegan Cheese

If you don't have time to create it from scratch, you can buy plant-based cheeses from most of the big supermarkets now. I have seen and tasted some incredible new cheeses that not only have a similar taste and texture to real cheese but have a rind around them. Others melt, so you won't have to give up the good old cheese toastie. There is also an amazing book out there called *This Cheese is Nuts* by Julie Piatt. She is the wife of Rich Roll, one of my plant-powered heroes (vegan triathlete, podcaster, author).

Cashew Parmesan

If this doesn't convince you that you don't need dairy in your life, then I don't know what will. If you love pasta then no doubt you lust after parmesan the way I once did, until I discovered this.

Once again, add a handful of dry cashews (other nuts will do and in fact hulled hemp seeds make an awesome nuttier version) to a blender with a pinch of salt (Himalayan or flaked sea salt are my favourites) and a generous handful of yeast flakes (use ones with added B12 for additional nutrition). Blend until you have a fine powder but stop before the mixture congeals. Nuts will release oils (nut butter) if you blend for too long and you want this mixture dry like dried parmesan.

Coconut Yoghurts

Lovely, luscious yoghurt made from the milk of the coconut. Free from dairy, soya, and gluten, but not temptation.

With so many dairy alternatives out there nowadays there really is no need to hang onto dairy, especially when you consider the health implications of a diet rich in milk and cheese but also the ethics and cruelty attached to the production of it.

So just let dairy go and along with it another barrier to the plant-powered lifestyle.

If we are trying to 'Reduce Trauma and Suffering' then we have to start letting go of dairy, it's better for our health, the animals and the environment.

CHAPTER RECIPE –

CASHEW, FIG AND VANILLA ICE CREAM

I loved ice cream, couldn't get enough of it on my treat days, but the first time I tried cashew nut ice cream I literally couldn't tell the difference and I wish I'd known about it for years.

If you have the time then of course soaking the nuts beforehand overnight or for a couple of hours is great but if not, it's not the end of the world. This recipe works because it's so simple and quick to make.

Servings: 2

Ingredients:

- 250 g organic cashews
- 3 organic figs
- 1 vanilla pod
- Nut milk (just enough so that it reaches a yoghurt-like consistency in blender/processor)

You will need:

- 1 blender or food processor
- 1 bowl and stirring spoon

Cooking Method:

1. Add the cashews, 1 fig and the inside of half a vanilla pod into a blender or food processor along with a small bit of nut milk. Blend until you have the consistency of yoghurt.

2. Chop up the 2 remaining figs and stir them into the mixture.
3. Add to a round-bottomed bowl (makes it easier to mix) and cover with cling film and put in the freezer. Then stir every 30 minutes and put back into the freezer, repeat this for 1.5–2 hours and it should be ready.

CHAPTER 9

VEGAN KITCHEN ESSENTIALS

The secret ingredient is always love.

To create tasty and nutritious plant-based recipes there are a few essential items to get hold of and stock in your cupboards. Alongside adding a generous helping of love, empathy and compassion to your cooking, these ingredients will take your flavours to a whole new level and fortify your meals with essential nutrients harder to obtain in a vegan diet.

Oils

Although we tend to cook with less and less oil in our household, usually cooking dishes with a blend of water and a little oil. My favourites oils to cook with that have a high smoking point are coconut, rice bran and avocado oil, and then extra virgin olive oil, flaxseed oil or sesame seed oil to dress dishes and salads with.

Yeast Flakes

Commonly known as 'Vegan Fish Food', it has a cheesy flavour and it provides a wealth of vitamins, minerals and protein. These are a must for anyone adopting a plant-based diet as they will not only add texture and flavour to your food but will help to add essential B vitamins into your diet which is harder to come by eating a vegan plant-based diet.

Some products are fortified with B12, that's the one to go for.

Miso Paste

Miso is a traditional fermented Japanese staple food and seasoning made from different types of grains but mainly soya and a unique koji fermentation culture. It can be found in white or dark varieties, white usually having a lower soya content. I love cooking with the dark version, as it adds real richness and depth to dishes, much the same as a stock cube but with a wider flavour profile.

Dried Seaweed

Another potential nutrient deficiency on a plant-based diet and in fact most diets is iodine. Iodine helps with the function of the thyroid which helps to control body temperature and metabolism. Iodine is also believed to provide antioxidants that may even help prevent heart disease and cancer.

The seaweeds soak up the natural salts found in the ocean making them a fantastic source of minerals. Nori, kombu and dulse are a few of the varieties available. Nori is the green sheets used to make sushi rolls. The Japanese have been drying and roasting this sea vegetable for 1,300 years.

One sheet of nori meets 70% of the daily value for iodine and 10% of the daily value for vitamin C. In addition to iodine and vitamin C, nori can also help you meet your daily needs for potassium, vitamin A and magnesium.

I love chopping a sheet of nori into thin slices and adding it to stocks and curries to give a fishy/sea flavour or for wrapping tofu to make 'tofish'.

Liquid Aminos

Liquid Aminos are a liquid seasoning very similar to tamari or soy sauce but unfermented. They provide a source of amino acids from soy or coconut and contain 16 of the 20 amino acids. Amino acids of course are the building blocks of protein, which we will discuss in more detail later in the book. It is always best to buy organic and non-GMO soy or soy ingredients where possible.

Tamari

Is traditionally used in Japanese cuisine versus the more common soy sauce used in Chinese. It is a thicker, less salty, fermented soy sauce that contains less wheat, and is often gluten-free. It can be used in Asian and non-Asian cooking to add a full, savoury, umami flavour to dishes.

Yeast Extract

As they say in the advert of a well-known brand "you either love it or hate it". I love it and especially so when spread on some rye toast then topped with mashed avocado – it's a flavour explosion! – or added to gravies and sauces to give a deep, rich meaty flavour.

Full of flavour and goodness and especially B vitamins along with added B12, a must for the cupboards. Again you'll find it in most supermarkets and health food stores.

Dairy-Free Pesto

You can obviously make it yourself easily with fresh ingredients but is great to have lying around in the fridge or cupboards, just to add that extra edge of flavour to a dish or dressing. You can find them mainly in the 'Free From' section in most supermarkets due to the dairy (parmesan cheese) found in traditional recipes and brands.

Or if you're feeling daring then you can make your own easily by adding the following ingredients together in a food processor:

- 2 cups of fresh basil
- ½ cup of pine nuts
- 1 clove fresh garlic

Then add the olive oil and salt until you have the right consistency and flavour.

- ¼ to ½ cup of extra virgin olive oil, as needed
- Sea salt to taste

Experiment with alternative herb and nut combinations for different flavours.

Blackstrap Molasses

This is a fantastic source of iron for those on a plant-based diet who might be lacking in this essential nutrient.

Blackstrap molasses is a rich source of the type of iron found in plant foods. One tablespoon of blackstrap molasses provides 3.5 mg of iron. This represents over 19% of the daily recommended amount of iron for adult women before menopause. It also contains over 43% of the daily recommended amount for adult men.

Blackstrap molasses can be added to many meals. An easy

way to boost your iron intake is to substitute white sugar or other sweeteners for blackstrap molasses. At breakfast, add blackstrap molasses to oatmeal or other hot cereal. Stir a spoonful of molasses into salad dressing at lunch and use it as a marinade. You can prepare a delicious substitute for hot tea or coffee by adding 1 tbsp of blackstrap molasses to one cup of hot water, soy milk or almond milk.

Top Tip: Vitamin C helps your body absorb iron from plant sources of iron such as blackstrap molasses. Try to eat foods high in vitamin C alongside blackstrap molasses. Citrus fruits and juices, cantaloupe, strawberries, sweet red peppers, tomatoes, cabbage and broccoli are all good choices.

Maple Syrup

Maple syrup is a great alternative to honey which is unfortunately not technically vegan. It is made from the sugary circulating fluid (sap) of maple trees. It has been consumed for many centuries in North America. Over 80% of the world's supply is now produced in Canada.

Like the contrast between whole and refined grains, unrefined natural sweeteners like maple syrup contain higher levels of beneficial nutrients, antioxidants and phytochemicals than white table sugar or high fructose corn syrup.

Dried Dates and Figs

Are a great way to add sweetness to smoothies or to chop up and have on porridge, salads, etc. You can also make a great honey alternative by blending a few dates and some water into a syrup.

Himalayan Sea Salt

This pink salt that is harvested naturally contains large quantities of essential minerals and is an essential addition to my kitchen, if you can't find Himalayan then go for flaked sea salt, another mineral-dense salt.

Nuts and Seeds

Having a good selection of different nuts and seeds will mean you can wiz up a quick snack, breakfast meal, jazz up a salad or finish off any meal with a crunch and added nutrients. Also, great to make your own cheese parmesan (as mentioned before) or to make homemade nut butters.

My favourite nuts are:

- **Cashews** – So versatile to make cashew cheese, cream or ice cream, they are fairly high in fat and carbohydrates so use sparingly if you're watching your calorie intake.
- **Brazil Nuts** – Best wholefood source of selenium, which is anti-inflammatory and helps lift the mood.
- **Walnuts** – Great source of omega 3, which in turn can help your heart health and mood. Also adds great texture to salads, on yoghurt or as a snack.
- **Pecan Nuts** – Because I love the taste of them, but they also help with heart health, inflammation, mood lifting and reducing oxidative stress.
- **Pistachio** – Alongside pecans as my two favourites, a fantastic dessert topping or as an ice cream flavour. They have also has been shown to reduce bad cholesterol and boost eye health.

My favourite seeds are:

- **Hemp Seeds** – Definitely my number one favourite of all seeds and plants, hemp is an amazing natural resource, utilised for fuel, healing with CBD oil, clothes, paper and other materials. There is literally no waste with hemp. But from a nutritional point of view hemp contains all the essential amino acids and is a fantastic source of omega 3 fats. In their shells they can be blended with water to make hemp milk or in their unshelled/dehulled form are fantastic in porridge, salad toppings, smoothies and just about anything else I can put them on.
- **Pumpkin Seeds** – Add great texture to dishes, topping for salads, and added to smoothies, they make a fantastic source of zinc, iron and protein.
- **Chia Seeds** – Great source of essential amino acids and omega 3 fats, one of my favourite super foods. Especially as they can be soaked in nut milk to make chia seed pudding, they soak up the liquid and create a jelly-like outer shell, very soothing for the digestive system.
- **Flaxseeds** – Another great source of omega 3 fat and a great way of making a 'vegan egg' that can be added as a binding agent to many dishes, such as nut loafs and burgers. Just soak 1 tbsp of ground flaxseed in 2.5 tbsp of water for 5 minutes, until it thickens.

Herbs

Fill your freezer with a few packs of different herbs that you can use at any time, such as basil, coriander, parsley, oregano, etc. Try the more fragrant Thai basil, it has a unique and incredible flavour perfect for curries and salads.

Nut Butter

You just can't beat a selection of nut butters to have in the cupboards – almond butter, cashew or peanut butter. They are great in smoothies, on fruit, in yoghurt or just as a calorie-dense snack, but go easy on them, they are calorific and super addictive. Also super easy to make at home in a food processor with any nut, it just takes 10–20 minutes of patience and voila.

Plant Protein Powder

I'm a big fan these days of plain unflavoured or vanilla organic protein powders. Plain or simple flavourings such as vanilla give you more diversity in use; you can always add berries or cacao for different flavours.

Now your cupboards are filled with plenty of awesome ingredients to help you concoct some super tasty and nutritious plant-powered meals and smoothies, you're well on your way to your new plant-powered life.

CHAPTER RECIPE

CHOC 'N' NUT PROTEIN BALLS

I've made and perfected this recipe for my Plant Powered Fitness cooking workshops and they always get a great reception when we tuck into them at the end of the day. I've also made them a few times at home, but beware... they are hard to resist!

Servings: 10–12 balls

Ingredients:

- 100 g almonds
- 60 g dried cranberries
- 60 g dates
- 60 g plant protein powder
- 40 g almond butter
- 30 g coconut oil
- 3 tbsp of water to bind

Topping

- 40 g vegan dark chocolate

You will need:

- 1 Magimix or food processor
- 1 mixing bowl

Cooking Method:

1. Melt the chocolate using a bain-marie. Bring a ¼ pan of water to the boil, place a glass bowl on top of the pan, making sure the bowl isn't touching the water,

and place your chocolate into the bowl in broken pieces.

2. While the chocolate is melting, place the almonds in your food processor and blend for up to a minute or until a flour forms and the nuts have crumbled.
3. Add the cranberries and dates and blend until they come together. Then add the rest of the ingredients until it forms into a sticky dough. **Note**: If it is still a bit crumbly add 1 tbsp of water to the mixture to help it stick.
4. Use your hands to roll the mixture out into balls, place on a baking tray or plate covered with baking paper. You will get 10–12 balls from this mix. I aim for 10 so that each ball is more filling.
5. Once the chocolate has melted, remove from the pan and heat. Dip the balls in the chocolate, covering about half of each ball, before placing them back onto the tray and then put them into the fridge or freezer until the chocolate has set.

Now try not to eat them all at once!

CHAPTER 10 – SUPER FOODS

"If you think the pursuit of good health is expensive and time consuming, try illness."
Lee Swanson

There seems to be a different 'super food' discovered every week these days. I've lost count of the number of times I've seen 'the highest antioxidant content than any other food on our planet' in marketing literature.

The reality is that ALL plant-based natural wholefoods are 'super'. These luxury items just contain a condensed number of nutrients compared with the standard food groups we consume.

My nan lived to the ripe old age of 93 and I am pretty sure that spirulina and goji berries never passed her lips once. That's not to say that I don't believe in them, far from it, but they are a luxury and you can live a long healthy life without them.

However, I feel as the nutrient quality of our soil is reduced by monocultured farming and the CO2 levels reduce the nutrient density in our plant foods, the importance for having access to nutrient-dense food groups is magnified, no matter what dietary approach you follow.

Could my nan have lived beyond 100 had she eaten a

plant-based diet for most of her life while supplementing her diet with the best super foods? I like to think so, that's why I include a few regular super foods in my diet; I don't go crazy, and base my choices on both nutrients, quality, flavour, texture and cost.

Here are a few of the superfoods I regularly use:

Matcha Green Tea

As far as superfoods go, matcha is up there as one of my most used. This green tea variant has been used for centuries by everyone from samurai to monks.

All green teas contain caffeine, but in much lower quantities than coffee. Because of this, matcha has less of an effect on the adrenal glands, which can sometimes lead to anxiety, nervousness or hypertension in those sensitive to caffeine. It does however contain an amino acid called L-Theanine which promotes the production of alpha waves in the brain and induces an alert, yet calm and relaxed state.

Matcha also contains a unique set of antioxidants called catechins, making up 60% of its entire antioxidant contents. This powerful, organic compound is known for its cancer-fighting properties and matcha contains over a hundred times as much catechin as other teas.

I love using matcha when I take a break from coffee and I also enjoy mixing it with medicinal mushroom powders such as cordyceps and reishi for an extra nutritional and energetic push.

Adaptogens

Adaptogens are a unique class of healing plants: they help balance, restore and protect the body. An adaptogen doesn't have a specific action; it helps you respond to any influence or stressor, normalising your physiological functions.

Cordyceps and Reishi (Chinese medicinal mushrooms)

These amazing Chinese medicinal mushrooms have adaptogenic effects.

Cordyceps are a genus of fungi that has been used in herbal medicine for centuries. The most interesting health benefits of cordyceps include its ability to improve respiratory health, increase oxygen uptake, boost heart health, detoxify the body and prevent certain types of cancer. It slows the ageing process, increases energy, and improves the immune system.

Reishi mushrooms are one of the most popular and beneficial types of fungi on the planet. These mushrooms have been relied upon for thousands of years in the Asian region. They boost energy, reduce blood pressure, slow the ageing process, and may prevent cancer. They also detoxify the body, eliminate inflammation and improve your cognitive ability.

Maca

Maca is an edible root native to the Andes of Peru. Maca is an adaptogen so it is great for hormonal balance, energy, mood and has a broad spectrum of amino acids, many vitamins, minerals and antioxidants. Great for adding into a post-workout smoothie to help rebalance the body.

Cacao (nibs and powder)

Different from cocoa powder, which is heated to high temperatures in roasting and loses much of its nutritional value, cacao is the raw version made from cold pressed unroasted cacao beans.

I love cacao, as a powder it is super versatile, you can add it into smoothies, porridge, baking, hot drinks, etc.

From a nutritional standpoint, some of the benefits include: lowers insulin resistance, protects the nervous system, lowers blood pressure, guards against toxins, boosts mood and contains high levels of essential minerals such as magnesium, iron, potassium, calcium, zinc, copper, manganese, along with antioxidants and fibre.

Cacao nibs are in an even more unprocessed form. They have a slightly higher caffeine content and are great in smoothies and porridge but I love to use them in chia seed puddings as they give a wonderfully rich, chocolaty crunch. Beware – eaten on their own they are quite bitter.

Spirulina

Spirulina is a blue-green algae grown around the world from Mexico to Africa. It is renowned for its intense flavour and even more powerful nutritional profile. If you've ever added spirulina to a smoothie it turns it bright green in seconds.

It detoxes heavy metals, improves gut bacteria, contains amino acids, iron and antioxidants and is great to drink during training for amino acids or in post-workout smoothies to help alkaline the digestive system.

Top Tip: Spirulina contains the amino acids glycine, arginine and methionine, which are used by the body to naturally create creatine, which is a very effective compound when looking to improve size, strength and performance in the gym. You cannot directly find it on a plant-based diet as it comes from meat in many cases or by supplementing a synthetic version. But if you consume spirulina before and/ or after a workout it will help to maximise the production and levels of creatine in the body naturally.

Chia, Hemp and Flax Seeds

I mentioned these in the nuts and seeds section earlier in the chapter, but they deserve to be listed under super foods due to their superior nutrient density and delicious addition to many dishes. They are a great source of fibre, omega 3 fats, high in antioxidants, amino acids, vitamins and minerals. These powerhouse seeds add protein, essential fats, and awesome textures to smoothies, porridge, salads, nut roasts and much more.

Baobab

Baobab is the fruit of Africa's 'Tree of Life'. It is the only fruit in the world that dries naturally on the branch.

It is also almost 50% fibre (two-thirds soluble and one-third insoluble, making it a powerful prebiotic) and is a great source of antioxidants. It is also high in vitamin C, which helps iron absorption, so is the perfect accompaniment in smoothies with leafy greens, pumpkin seeds and other plant-based sources of iron. It adds a slight citrus tang to a smoothie.

Goji

Also known as wolfberries, goji berries have long been enjoyed in China and the Himalayas for their sweet taste and bright colour. Their history as a medicinal plant has roots in ancient China, where goji berries still are used to treat eye, liver and kidney ailments.

These tasty little dried berries offer a unique texture and flavour to puddings, salads or are great on their own as a snack.

Goji berries are high in vitamin C and fibre, and low in calories. They are also a good source of iron, vitamin A and are high in antioxidants, with some studies showing they help with inflammatory diseases and may also help with anti-ageing and degenerative diseases.

Great topping on porridge, chia puddings and, as I found out, for making the fermented drink kefir.

CHAPTER RECIPE

SUPER CHIA PUDDING

This makes a lovely creamy breakfast and I find it very soothing on the digestive system first thing in the morning. Its texture and look when soaked maybe likened to frog spawn but it goes well when combined with smooth creamy non-dairy yoghurt, tangy berries and the crunchier textures of seeds and cacao nibs. I love making this the night before or in the morning to take with me if I'm in a hurry.

Servings: 1

Ingredients:

- 40 g chia seeds
- 200 ml nut milk

Topping

- 2 tbsp flaked coconut
- 2 tbs of non-dairy yoghurt
- 1 tbsp shelled hemp seeds
- 1 tbsp pumpkin seeds
- 1 tbsp cacao nibs
- 1 tbsp goji berries
- 1 handful of berries (raspberries and/or blueberries)

You will need:

- 1 serving bowl
- 1 spoon to stir and eat with

Cooking Method:

1. You can either soak the chia seeds overnight with the nut milk, which I do if I'm going to be in a hurry in the morning, or you can soak them for about 15–20 minutes while you get in the shower.

Top Tip: After you've added the nut milk to the chia seeds, give them a good stir and leave them for a minute and then come back and give them another good stir. Do this one more time. This prevents them from turning into a solid lump and keeps them in a nice smooth porridge-like consistency when you come to eat them.

Now add all the toppings, starting with the biggest to the smallest; so first the yoghurt, then the coconut flakes, then the berries, etc. This just makes it look good, so you can post it on social media.

SUMMARY

You should now have a very good understanding as to:

- Why I've written this book.
- Why you should read on and follow me further on this plant-powered journey.
- The basics you need to know to begin your own transition from meat to plants.
- Just remember as you embark on your own plant-powered quest, the following points from this first section of discovery that I made.

- **Find Your WHY** – Having a strong why or reason for change is so important to begin with. It's this strong emotional anchor as to why you are choosing a new set of behaviours in your life; it's this strong heartfelt emotional anchor that will carry you through the more challenging times when you can't find anything to eat in a supermarket or while out in a restaurant with friends; it will also carry you through the swathes of negativity that may come your way from friends, family and the mainstream media. Think of your WHY as that bright light to focus on at the end of the tunnel, it is your hope and faith in building a better world.

- **Be The Change** – Remember that NOTHING changes unless YOU first put the work in to change first. Change always starts from within and the most effective way to bring change to the lives of all those around you is to live your own life openly with integrity, authenticity, empathy and compassion. Everyone will feel the positive energy emanating from you, in your thoughts, words and actions, which will make them ask why and how.

- **Progress Not Perfection** – Aim for perfection but embrace the fact that you'll never get there. Perfection doesn't exist, life is full of both dark, light, positive and negative, so instead work on progressing and just making your life and your contribution that little bit better every day.

  Stop being so hard on yourself and lean into this new lifestyle. Try a little bit here, a little bit there, read, listen and learn about the myriad of benefits that come when you bring more plants and nature into your life.

  It's better to do a little bit here and there, rather than nothing at all. Start with one vegan meal, then one vegan day and build it slowly so that it doesn't feel overwhelming. If you end up after six months still consuming animal products two days a week but were once consuming them for seven, then fantastic, you've made a massive difference. Life is a journey of constant process and evolution towards improvement.

  No one ever learnt to run before they could walk.

- **Don't Judge** – If you ate meat for 30 years of your life and have just turned vegan for the last six months, then who are you to judge others who have not found the path yet and are where you once were? Don't judge them and come across 'holier than thou', listen to them and empathise with where they are, use your experience of how you made the change and offer constructive and supportive information and advice.

- **Reduce Trauma and Suffering** – Whichever reason you ultimately choose for switching to a plant based diet, I'm sure you'll agree that knowing your actions are helping to reduce trauma and suffering will make you feel much lighter, I don't think any of us really want to intentionally create more of it on this planet, there's plenty already.

Now let's look at how to Transform Your Body…

PART 2

PLANT-POWERED FITNESS

Part 1 of this book was about my own journey and how you can start making the change. In Part 2 we are going to look into the journey of transforming your body, and the foundational elements that need to be in place, whether you are on a plant-based diet or not. You will see that eating a plant-based diet really doesn't change any of the fundamental laws of body transformation you need to abide by, the same rules still apply.

The lessons in this chapter have been learnt through my personal and professional experience, through the successful application of these techniques and external courses and studies that I have completed over the years.

Having read Part 1 you'll remember just how many times I've taken my own body through physical transformations, in modelling, through illness and for fitness shows. These principles have also been applied to many coaching clients over the years.

After I went vegan and was working my way into the lifestyle, I had to question whether I could apply the same principles that I'd been using for years relating to training and nutrition.

- Would I be able to achieve the same results?
- Would a plant-based diet sustain my training and recovery?
- Could I manipulate carbohydrates, fats and proteins as I had done on a meat-based diet?

The answer to all those questions I found out through my

own self experimentation was a resounding YES!

I realised that not only could I transform my body internally and externally, but I could also have a huge impact on animals and the planet at the same time. This was an exciting realisation and would now add extra meaning and motivation for getting into great shape, as it was no longer just about my body and my own personal reasons for getting into shape, but it took on a much greater meaning beyond my own immediate world.

Whenever you focus on getting into great shape on a plant-based vegan diet you are no longer just doing it for yourself, but for the animals and the environment as well. This adds an extra element of motivation during challenging times when you need to focus and push through a workout or stick to your plan.

There's no better way to educate and to show others what is possible to achieve than by showing it with your own actions and results, which gets attention in the world of fitness and bodybuilding, helping to raise awareness.

CHAPTER 11

THE SAME RULES APPLY

"From small hinges
you can swing big doors."
Tim Ferriss

Do vegans need to work out differently?
Can you get strong on a plant-based diet?
Can you add muscle without meat?

The documentary *The Game Changers*, which was released in 2019, did a great job of answering these questions but they are still concerns that I hear regularly. So just to put it to bed now, the same rules apply whether you eat meat or plants, and in this chapter, we will go over some of the key requirements when it comes to getting into shape, no matter what kind of diet you espouse to.

The key golden nugget of information to remember is that you can make big changes happen in your body and life, by just making small but deliberate changes to the way you live, eat, sleep and train.

There's No Magic Pill

I thought we'd dispel this myth first, as it is the first stumbling block that I made myself and that any new and eager fitness enthusiast makes. We want results, but we want results fast, like yesterday, and therefore tend to look for a much easier route to the body you've always desired. We are so influenced by social media these days and the finished product that people display but we don't see the months and years of hard work that have gone into creating that result.

The overnight success that was ten years in the making.

Don't get me wrong, there are ways we can speed up the process, making everything more efficient, increasing the positive impact on our bodies with the quality of the food we eat and the way we train, so that we get a bigger bang for our buck. But there are NO short cuts. Hard consistent effort in and out of the training environment works every time.

The sooner you realise that as a lifter, the sooner you can get to work and avoid wasting time and money on unnecessary supplements or fitness 'hocus pocus'.

I remember when I first started on this physical journey back when I was 19, I read a *Muscle and Fitness* magazine and was totally sold by an advert for a box of high protein meal replacements sachets and a couple of other 'must have' supplements. I spent £60 of my hard-earned cash on these products, and I remember placing so much hope on the purchase of these 20 sickly strawberry meal replacement sachets, thinking they were going to magically turn my body into a similar one as the model on the advert overnight. I didn't realise that they would last less than two weeks and I would need to keep buying more.

Now 20 years on from that time in my life I realise how much money I've spent on supplements over the years, some necessary and effective but many were not.

First lesson learnt. Constant application in every aspect will be needed, this is a life-long journey, you don't just transform your body once and that's it, but you will probably go through many of these transformations over the years. So without sounding clichéd it really is important to enjoy the journey, the process and not just the destination, because the destination is a constantly evolving point in time, which changes as you do.

In 2013 I decided to try out two different approaches to supplementing while competing for the WBFF Denmark and WBFF London fitness model shows. For the WBFF Denmark show in April 2013 I threw every supplement that I thought would benefit me at the process (all legal) and I did get into great shape, at the time my best. I measured, monitored and diligently recorded everything that I did.

Then later that year for the WBFF London show in November I decided not to take any supplements apart from the standard protein powder, some creatine, vitamins and minerals. I also adopted the most relaxed approach to the show prep that I ever had. I ate a very nutrient-diverse diet, which I still monitored and calculated, but due to the more relaxed nature and the increased nutrient diversity, it was the most enjoyable show prep I had ever done and I got into even better shape than previously in the year. This was partly due to my experience, understanding my body and knowing how it would respond, but it definitely made me reflect on the importance that I had been placing on supplements and how much of the beneficial effects we feel from them actually come from the placebo effect.

It also highlighted to me the need to train and eat smarter not harder, and to work with the body rather than forcing it.

Supplements should always be viewed as just that, a supplement to a good dietary approach and structured training programme. I still use them but only the ones that give me the most 'progress for my pound' and these days I spend more of my money on good food and natural super foods before sport supplements. If you support the body with all its natural requirements to perform and recover, then it generally will.

Avoid Programme Hopping

One of the limiting factors I've seen for years with clients and myself when I first started out was the temptation to hop from one programme to the next before you start feeling or seeing results.

One week you read an article in *Muscle and Fitness* magazine for the best bulging biceps workout ever, then the following week you read an article and workout in *Men's Health* that promises 'Arms like Arnie', so you then find yourself hopping from one to the other in an attempt to fast track your results. But both programmes require you to focus on them separately and see them through to the end. This advice is for the ladies as well, female fitness magazines and glute/butt workouts are all the rage now, so beware!

Most programmes will work, as long as you do.

Every time I take my body on another transformational journey I am constantly reminded of just how slowly results come and that you just have to keep chipping away with each rep, each set, each workout, each day, each week and each month. When you look back at your progress three months down the line, it feels like it's all happened quite quickly but in truth every day you've been grinding away and making small changes to your physique that build up over an extended period of time.

What doesn't help is that once we are on that path, our focus is on our body and the changes it's making; change happens slowly yet we monitor our progress regularly, and we see very little change, becoming disheartened.

So, work out your goals, find a suitable programme and see it through from start to finish. You will learn a lot about your body every time you complete a programme, as much when it doesn't work as when it does, giving you a greater understanding of the best way to get results for you. This is a lifelong journey that constantly evolves as your body does.

Consistency and Commitment

As the saying goes, 'Rome Wasn't Built in a Day' and neither was a fit, athletic, healthy physique, and the length of time needed to get there depends on a few factors:

- **Starting Point** – How far have you let your health or body slip, how long have you been making poor health choices, have you been ill or maybe injured?

- **Expectations** – What is your expectation of what you'd like to achieve, do you just want to improve your health and not run out of breath walking up the stairs, lose a few pounds and fit into those jeans or are you looking to build a body like a magazine cover model, improve your performance for a team sport, or crush that next CrossFit workout?
- **Consistency** – How consistent can you be every day, applying behavioural habits and actions, sustained over a prolonged period?
- **Commitment** – How long are you willing to commit to the process, in both time and effort to achieve your goals?

Imagine there's a scale representing the balance between successfully completing your goal or failing to do so. On one side of the scale there is Expectation and on the other side Commitment.

Now if your Expectations are too high in comparison to the effort you're willing to put in on the Commitment side, then you're probably not going to realise your goal, so either your Expectations need to come down or your Commitment level needs to go up. It's that simple, how much do you want it?

You then need to apply these factors consistently, every day over a long period of time, gradually chipping away at your goal. Whenever I start a transformation of my own it's always a wake-up call when I realise how slow and gradual the changes come. That is why it's so important that your Expectations match your Commitment, as it's this balance of visualisation and energy that will determine your ultimate success.

Focus on Frequency over Intensity

One of the more destructive phrases to ever come into the gym and get promoted on social media is 'Go Hard or Go Home', giving everyone the impression that they must train at 100% intensity every time or they are weak individuals who should just not bother at all. This, as you will see throughout this book, is a problematic perspective for humans when it comes to creating positive change.

The athlete who trains at 100% intensity every time he or she goes into the gym will not maintain the same level of consistency throughout the year as an athlete who trains at 70% every time.

Over the course of the year, that 70% athlete will have less injuries, less time out due to fatigue and will have accumulated a greater amount of training volume, thus progression towards their goals, than the athlete who 'goes hard or goes home' every time they hit the gym. This is because the more sessions they train at 100% intensity, the less overall training volume they will achieve and the more likely they are to stay home and not actually make it to the gym.

That's why you don't find athletes hitting their 1RMs and personal bests leading up to a competition. They leave that FOR the competition.

Of course, every so often it's essential to go all in and have a few 100% intensity sessions but not every day or every session, these periods should be tapered and built up to. Knowing when to push and when to back off is critical to your long-term success. If you were to create a visual representation of how your training intensity should look then a wave of sound would be ideal, going from high to low intensity and back to high, in a nice smooth curve rather than an abrupt straight line. This gives the body both the stimulation it needs and the recovery it needs to adapt. This is also known as 'periodisation' in the coaching world, the planning of different training phases that focus on the gradual alteration of intensity, volume and/or frequency.

Remember reduced intensity will lead to greater frequency in training overall, this is a long game not a short game.

Use it or Lose it

The human body is the most efficient and lazy machine on the planet, always looking for the path of least resistance. Building and maintaining muscle has a high-energy cost, and your body is always looking to expend the least amount of energy to maintain 'homeostasis', or metabolic balance within the body.

If you're not providing the appropriate level of stimulation to your body then you will gradually lose the gains you have achieved, as it reverts to what is absolutely necessary for survival. Of course the older your training age (length of years exercising/training) then the easier it is for you to get back to where you were before, but you have to put the hard graft in at some point to get there.

Change Workout Variables

In terms of weightlifting you should alter the variables and the way you're lifting weights every three to six workouts by changing the sets, reps, tempo, rest, angles, grip thickness, etc.

Sometimes all you need to change is the speed and explosive nature with which you lift the weights. This will recruit and engage different muscle fibres that your body has been using to lift a given weight. By changing one of the above variables you will give your body a new set of stressors to adapt to.

For endurance sports, the workout variables you could change would be speed, time and training frequency.

If you don't give your body anything new to adapt to then it won't adapt, that's a fact and it reminds me of the Einstein quote...

> *"The definition of insanity is repeating the same thing over again, whilst expecting a different result."*

Remember if you don't change, then nothing else will. This law can be applied to every aspect of your life, it's an important lesson to learn and one we have already touched upon in terms of 'being the change we wish to see in the world' and we will revisit before this book has ended.

Tell the World and be Accountable

Finding your personal motivation by cultivating a strong why is essential to the process but sometimes it's still not enough and we benefit greatly from holding ourselves accountable to others, friends, family, strangers or our own coach.

For some reason we are more likely to let ourselves down rather than other people and this is where accountability becomes a very strong motivational force to harness.

Back in the day whenever I decided to take part in a fitness show I would talk about it openly on social media, and I would also let colleagues and those closest to me know what my plans were. Then I'd pay my entrance fee for the show which would further commit myself to the process.

My reason was that by telling as many people as I could, I made it hard, if not impossible, to go back on my word. I used the knowledge that I'm quite stubborn to help keep me accountable. Also, knowing that you're going to be standing on stage in a pair of tight pants in front of a big audience would complete the motivational process.

If your goals don't scare you, they aren't big enough.

CHAPTER RECIPE

MISO NOODLE SOUP AND BAKED TOFU

This is such an exceptionally tasty, simple and nutritious dish. I love the satisfying texture of the udon noodles and the crispy chunks of tofu. If ever I'm feeling a bit run-down, then this kind of dish with all the fresh ingredients – especially the ginger and garlic – really gives my immune system a boost.

Once I discovered baked tofu, I fell in love with the stuff. The baked tofu cubes are great stored in the fridge and used on salads or as a high-protein snack.

Servings: 1

Ingredients:

- 200 g/1 pack of firm tofu
- 100 g udon noodles
- 2 sliced mushrooms
- 1 carrot chopped into diagonal thin slices
- 1 small handful of broccoli florets
- 1 onion chopped
- 1 fresh clove of garlic
- 1 fresh piece of ginger (thumb size)
- ½ a leek
- ½ a red sweet pepper
- 1 tbsp dark miso
- 1 tbsp apple cider vinegar
- 3 tbsp tamari

- 1 tsp sesame oil
- Season with pepper

You will need:

- 1 large pan with lid
- 1 wooden spoon
- 1 sharp knife
- 1 chopping board
- 1 serving bowl

Cooking Method:

1. Drain and then slice a block of firm tofu into 3 even slices, then turn it to the side and make 3 more slices, then turn it over and make another 3 even slices, so that you now have lots of little cubes of tofu.
2. Toss the tofu in 2 tbsp of tamari and 1 tsp of sesame oil. Preheat the oven to a high heat and then throw in the tofu on a non-stick baking tray or some foil to bake for 10–15 minutes. Keep an eye on them as they don't take long to brown. Take them out after 5–10 minutes and move them around to make sure they aren't sticking and so they get a more all-over crust. Just bake long enough so they are firm and browned.
3. While the tofu is cooking add 1 tsp of coconut oil and add a little water to the pan to speed up the cooking. Sauté the chopped onion, chopped garlic, the ginger sliced into match sticks or small pieces, half a sliced leek, 1 tbsp dark miso, and put the lid back on and just allow some of the aromas to come out.
4. Then add the carrot chopped into diagonal thin slices, sliced mushrooms, half a red sweet pepper, small handful of broccoli florets, 1 tbsp apple cider vinegar,

1 tbsp tamari, and season with pepper.

5. Now fill the pan with enough boiling water so that it will cover the 100 g of udon noodles and add the noodles.
6. Once the noodles have cooked through serve the soup in a deep bowl, top with the baked tofu cubes, 2 sliced spring onions and a sprinkling of sesame seeds, then drizzle with hot sauce to taste, a dash of tamari and sesame seed oil to finish.

Now that's a Seriously Big Delicious Bowl of Plant Power to enjoy!

CHAPTER 12

GOAL SETTING

"Motivation gets you going and habit gets you there."
Zig Ziglar

The first step in setting your goal is to first work out where the destination is and what this looks like, then work back from that point.

I always ask prospective clients what their Ultimate Fitness Goal is. Asking someone to really think hard and simplify what their Ultimate Fitness Goal is will help them to really focus on that one thing without being distracted; it's that driving factor that you can keep coming back to when you need to steer the ship back on course.

Visualise the Destination

It's important to be honest and superficial if you need to, so that you can visualise in your mind's eye how that destination will look. The goal is specific to you, so whatever it is that you want to change; lose belly fat, increase arm size, a bigger butt, run a half marathon, walk up the stairs without being out of breath, etc.

The goal can be anything, but it must be specific to enable that visualisation process, just being fitter and healthier aren't specific enough.

Anchor to your Emotions

The next step is to focus on how you would feel if you woke up tomorrow morning having achieved that goal overnight. Emotional anchors give us a strong WHY, a deeper reason for working towards that goal. Having a Visual and Emotional representation of your goal in your mind will really help you to start manifesting it into reality by giving you inner belief that you will achieve it. Once you strongly believe that you're going to achieve the goal, you're literally halfway there; it's just a matter of when rather than if.

This destination is called your Outcome Goal.

Set a Course

Once you have a destination or Outcome Goal to aim for, you just need to work out how to get there by setting yourself a course.

If you were the captain of a ship and you needed to set sail to a faraway land, you wouldn't just set off from the port without having an idea of where and what your destination looked like, and the route that you needed to take to get there (unless of course you are an intrepid explorer going where no man has gone before).

As a ship's captain you would set a course to your destination, the best route possible but you would also remain flexible in knowing that along the way there might be poor weather conditions and other potential hazards that would cause you to alter your course, going around the object, before getting back on track.

Well goal setting is much the same for life and body transformations. Sometimes life gets in the way, work can pile up, you might have family responsibilities, you may have slept poorly the night before, etc. There are a million things that are out of our control on a daily basis and there will always be bumps in the road. As long as you expect and accept this will happen then you can navigate these challenges with minimal disruption, letting go of the process knowing that once you've cleared the obstacle you will get back on track.

Always work towards Progress not Perfection, you're a human being, not a machine.

We have total control over what goes into our ears and our mouths.

Monitor Progress Regularly

Having set sail into the wide-open seas, with little more than the horizon to guide you on all sides, you would need to regularly monitor your progress using a compass and a map to ensure that you were on track and not floating off around the world in the opposite direction or falling off the edges. We have GPS these days of course, but you get my point; the GPS system still needs a Destination so that it can work out your best route. Think of your coach or personal trainer as a GPS system.

We must always first set an Outcome Goal and then regularly monitor progress towards that goal, using photos, measurements, fitness tests and blood tests, etc. to guide us and to feedback the effectiveness of our behavioural habits, such as lifestyle changes, training programmes, nutrition intake, sleep routines and other daily habits.

Here's a couple of examples of where monitoring progress can help:

- **Calorie Counting** – Is not always necessary for most people but more suitable for those in search of a more extreme physical goal. If you want to lose weight or body fat you MUST be in a calorie deficit, eating less energy than you are expending.

  You need to consume the right amount of energy for your bodyweight or the bodyweight you want to become, but as you lose weight then your metabolic/calorie needs will also change. So to prevent a plateau in progression, regular monitoring and fine tuning of your training volume and energy intake will be needed to keep you on track.

  You may also need to count calories if you're performing lots of endurance work to ensure that you are refuelling the body to help with recovery after long workouts.

- **Workout Variation** – Along with your energy and metabolic needs changing throughout the process, so will the stimulus that your body requires to adapt and change.

  Monitoring progress using fitness tests, photos and measurements will give you signs as to whether your body is reacting to the stimulus being placed on it by the current training programme. This gives you invaluable information so that you can either try something new or keep tweaking the body along the same lines.

- **Blood Tests** – If improved overall health or specific blood markers are your goals then taking a blood test every three months will help give you an idea as to whether the nutrition and/or supplement regime you're on is working for you, progressing you to improved health and ensuring that you're not deficient in essential nutrients. Handy for those on a plant-Based diet to monitor any potential deficiencies (to be continued later).

Outcome Goals vs Behavioural Goals

As we discussed earlier in this chapter, your Outcome Goal is your Ultimate Fitness Goal, that visualisation, the deep emotional anchor and the destination you want your body to finally end up at.

Your Outcome Goal is an essential start and end to the process, it's the big picture that carries your vision but is useless without also setting behavioural goals/habits as well, these are the details.

I like to use the analogy of the Outcome Goal as a brick wall that we are trying to build.

The brick wall standing alone is a solid, well-finished structure but it wasn't like that as it was being built. It was under construction, messy some days, cement everywhere, bricks exposed, it didn't always look so great but was undergoing a necessary process of growth, which doesn't always look clean and tidy, but the brick wall would never exist without that process.

Our behavioural habits and goals are the cement and bricks that make up the wall. A single brick on its own doesn't look significant but when hundreds of them are all placed on top and side by side, linked to one another, then they become that strong well-finished structure.

Behavioural habits and goals are the actions we apply daily that accumulate to achieve our Outcome Goal; such as preparing our food for the next day, getting to bed and sleeping seven to nine hours, eating three unrefined wholefood plant-based meals per day, working out intensely four times per week, drinking plenty of water, etc. Of course, the behavioural habits that you adopt must be in alignment with your Outcome Goal.

Without our daily behavioural habits, the outcome goal would never come to fruition, the brick wall would just remain a nice visualisation unrealised in this physical reality.

It is the small seemingly insignificant actions we take every day, week or month that over a prolonged period accumulate to achieve our goals and dreams. No matter what they are, the details are important.

So, once you have worked out what your Outcome Goal is, all you need to do is reverse engineer it and break it down into manageable chunks, working on it bit by bit, embracing the process of growth and change.

Just make sure EVERYDAY is a NO ZERO DAY,
every little bit counts, don't give up, keep going.

CHAPTER RECIPE

TOFISH, CHIPS AND MUSHY PEAS

Think of that final beautiful, delicious plate of tofish, chips and mushy peas as an Outcome Goal and all the elements that make it up as the Behavioural Habits; the tofu, nori, potato, peas, etc. all on their own quite plain and insignificant, until you prepare them, flavour them and combine them.

Servings: 2

Ingredients:

- 4 big potatoes
- 1 block of firm tofu
- Nori sheets
- Tamari
- Extra virgin olive oil
- Frozen organic peas
- Non-dairy cream
- Salt and pepper

You will need:

- 1 sharp knife
- 1 potato peeler
- 1 chopping board
- 1 baking tray

Cooking Method:

Prepare the oven chips first

1. Take the potatoes and cut into chips, then par boil them for 10 minutes. They won't need long as they are quite thin, and you don't want them to fall apart, so keep an eye on them.
2. Drain the chips and then toss them in a little olive oil, salt, pepper and any other herbs and spices at this stage.
3. Then place on a non-stick baking tray or a baking tray lined with foil and place in the oven for about 30 minutes.

Then prepare the tofish

1. Drain the block of tofu, cut into 4 pieces (2 pieces per person) and then place in a bowl marinating them in tamari.
2. Then cut the nori sheets to size for the tofu and roll the tofu up in the nori. This will give it that flavour of the sea and a crispy outer texture.
3. Then place the tofish on a baking tray with the nori sheet join down and bake the tofu for 20–30 minutes at 200°C, turning every 10 minutes so that it doesn't stick. Once the nori is crispy and the tofu firm, it is ready to eat.

Mushy Peas

1. Boil the organic frozen peas until just cooked.
2. Then mash the peas and season with salt, pepper and a dash of non-dairy cream. You could use shop-bought soy or oat cream, or maybe make your own using cashews.

Now plate up all three elements and watch your delicious

Outcome Goal come together. The meaty texture of the tofu goes so well with the crispy chips and the creamy mushy peas.

I can't tell you how satisfying this meal is – enjoy!

CHAPTER 13
THE DOUBLE DS

"Everything in moderation, including moderation."
Gramps

After you've assessed your levels of consistency, commitment and expectation and have set out your outcome and behavioural goals, the next step in the process of improving your health, body composition and performance is to make sure your body has all the necessary nutritional ingredients to support your training, recovery and vitality.

Ensuring your diet is both nutritionally diverse and nutritionally dense is essential for anyone wishing to experience optimal health and to avoid deficiencies, especially for those on a plant-based diet.

I find the deeper I go with plant-powered nutrition and this vegan life, focusing more and more on natural wholefoods, superfoods and avoiding refined foods as much as possible, the healthier I feel, the more connected with my body and the stronger the energy flows.

Nutrient Diversity

There is always so much focus in the media on the potential deficiencies while on a plant-based diet. While this may be somewhat true, it is also true if you're eating animal products. Most people are starving of nutrients as opposed to calories, due to a lack of time, opting for convenience over nutrient diversity.

The easiest way to avoid many nutritional deficiencies is by adopting a diet that is diverse in many different foods, fruits and vegetables.

You've heard the phrase 'eat the rainbow' right? Well that is a very visual and simple way of making sure you are eating a diverse diet, by trying to eat as many different coloured fruits and vegetables as you can.

Each different coloured fruit or vegetable has a different composition of nutrients, so by simply selecting as many different colours as you can find, you are ensuring a diverse pool of nutrients at your body's disposal.

Nutrient Density

It's very easy to eat a calorie-dense diet, even as a vegan. Calorie-dense food groups are those that have a higher ratio of calories relative to their volume (the amount of space that a substance or object occupies); most of the time these are denser higher fat foods such as nuts, nut butters, oils and avocados.

I'm not labelling these foods 'bad', just that they should be eaten in moderation, as they make it too easy to consume a vast number of energy/calories with just a few mouthfuls.

As an example, 500 calories of oil would have a much different volume and satiating effect than 500 calories of broccoli. It would take you longer to consume 500 calories of broccoli due to the fibre and overall food volume than it would the oil.

This shows you that it is all too easy to overeat calorie-dense foods and that the more nutrient-dense foods you consume, not only will you feel full for longer, but you will receive a much greater level of nutrients at your disposal for optimising your health and performance.

VEGAN MYTH BUSTING
YOU WILL BE DEFICIENT IN NUTRIENTS ON A PLANT-BASED DIET

OK, firstly just because you eat animal products doesn't necessarily mean that you'll not be deficient in at least three different nutrients.

A study published in the *Journal of the International Society of Sports Nutrition* showed that it's difficult to get all the essential vitamins and minerals from food alone and how common nutrient deficiencies are, no matter which diet you choose to eat. The study analysed 70 athlete diets, all of which were deficient in at least three nutrients, and we're not even talking vegan diets alone here. Some diets were missing up to 15 nutrients. The most common deficiencies:

- iodine
- vitamin D
- zinc
- vitamin E
- calcium

With regards a vegan diet, B12 really is the only nutrient that you can't get from a natural plant food source, unless you ate soil regularly which I don't recommend. As a vegan you need to boost your intake in the form of fortified foods or supplements. Luckily there are many foods out there such as marmite, nutritional yeast, nut milks, etc. that are fortified with B12 and many other vitamins and minerals such as vitamin D, calcium, magnesium, zinc and iron.

DHA (from Omega 3s), iron, zinc, iodine and vitamin D3 are other main potential deficiencies but not with a properly structured and nutrient-dense approach.

It always amazes me when I hear the anti-vegan arguments about having to take a B12 supplement every now and then, when many people are probably already taking a vitamin C tablet, some fish oils, a protein supplement and maybe even a multivitamin. Why are they then suddenly concerned about taking supplements?

The reality of soil degradation and climate change effecting nutrient quality (CO2 levels are affecting nutrient density in plants) means that most people will take a supplement of some sort, either a fortified food, super food or direct supplement, whether you're on a vegan diet or not.

Let's briefly touch on protein as it seems to be on everyone's lips. In the Western world we are eating on average four times more protein than we need anyway, especially if you eat meat several times a day. You just don't need as much as you think and while protein is essential (more so for specific people requiring recovery and enhanced performance), so are the 24 or more ESSENTIAL vitamins and minerals that your body requires. (We will be discussing protein at much greater length later in this book.)

So before making wild assumptions about a vegan diet being deficient in nutrients, go and get yourself tested first. You might be surprised what you're lacking in.

A well-balanced nutrient-dense plant-based diet probably provides MORE nutrients overall than any other diet, because the focus is on a diverse range of fruits and vegetables as a baseline, rather than the central focus on a plate being a piece of animal protein.

CHAPTER RECIPE

MIXED BERRY SMOOTHIE BOWL

One of my favourite ways to get a big boost of nutrients through a very quick, simple and delicious meal is through the smoothie bowl made with frozen berries and a few other super food ingredients.

The berries and dark chocolate will provide you with a big boost of antioxidants, the plant protein, hemp, chia, pumpkin seeds and coconut flakes will add plenty of protein and essential fats.

Servings: 1

Ingredients:

- 200 g frozen berries
- 1 scoop plant-based protein powder
- 20 g shelled hemp seeds
- 20 g pumpkin seeds
- 20 g coconut flakes
- 10 g chia seeds
- 10 g/1 square of dark chocolate (70% cacao or more) finely chopped
- Non-dairy milk

You will need:

- 1 x blender (the Magimix is my preferred choice to make this dish)
- 1 x serving bowl (get yourself some coconut bowls if you want to make it Instagramable)

Cooking Method:

1. Add the frozen berries, plant protein powder, hemp, chia and pumpkin seeds into the blender or food processor adding non-dairy milk just to loosen up the ingredients. Add a little at a time; if you add too much liquid it will turn into a smoothie rather than the thicker consistency of a smoothie bowl.
2. Serve in a bowl and top with the coconut flakes and the finely chopped dark chocolate.

CHAPTER 14

ENERGY BALANCE

"Regardless of your caloric intake, you should never be in a nutrient deficit."
Muscle Nerds

Energy balance is critical to maintaining a healthy metabolism and body composition. It is this balance of energy that will affect whether the body is increasing or decreasing body fat and/or muscle mass.

Before we go any further let's just make sure you understand calorie basics. A calorie is a unit of potential energy contained within a macronutrient (proteins, fats and carbohydrates). This is measured using a piece of equipment called a 'bomb calorimeter', which measures the units of potential energy released by a food group, when set alight to heat water by 1 degree, giving the calorie/energy content of the food.

Energy In vs Energy Out
Think of energy balance as a pair of kitchen scales; on one side we have Energy In and on the other Energy Out:

- **Energy In** – Energy (calories) ingested through the food and drink we consume.

  If Energy In exceeds Energy Out then we are in Positive

Energy Balance with weight gain a potential outcome.

- **Energy Out** – Energy (calories) expended through metabolic processes and activity.

  If Energy Out exceeds Energy In we are in a Negative Energy Balance with weight loss a potential outcome.

Understanding this law is an essential part of understanding metabolism and how energy balance affects your health, body composition and performance and it's a law that exists whether you eat meat or plants. Everything is energy once it is broken down from its original form.

The Five Components of your Metabolism
Your metabolism is the sum of all the chemical reactions in the body along with the energy produced and expended through its various functions. Again, whether you eat meat or plants, your biology is the same.

Your overall metabolism or metabolic rate can be summed up by the following five metabolic components that utilise energy throughout the body:

- **BMR – Basal Metabolic Rate**
  This is the measure of energy used by your body to undertake the most vital functions in the body.

- **RMR – Resting Metabolic Rate**
  This is the sum of energy expended by your body during rest.

- **TEF – Thermic Effect of Feeding**
  This is the measure of energy your body uses daily to digest, absorb and assimilate the food you eat, which can be up to 10% of the daily energy expenditure.

- **NEAT – Non-Exercise Activity Thermogenesis**
  This is the amount of energy your body expends to perform everyday activities such as walking up the stairs or doing the washing up.

- **Exercise Activity**
  In active individuals they may expend up to 30% of their daily energy expenditure through exercise, maybe more depending on the length and intensity of the sessions.

So now we have a good understanding of how energy flows in and out of the body (in terms of calories) and what metabolism relates to, we can start to think about which components we can manipulate and stimulate to get the desired effect to help with body composition.

The first two BMR (Basal Metabolic Rate) and RMR (Resting Metabolic Rate) are indicators of a healthy and optimally functioning metabolism and are stimulated by both Energy In and Energy Out.

NOTE: When calorie intake is low, the amount needed to maintain a normally functioning RMR decreases. This occurs due to lowering of thyroid hormone output, reduced TEF and reduced muscle mass. When calorie intake is increased above daily needs, then RMR increases.

Do Calories Matter?

Ultimately yes, you MUST be in a calorie DEFICIT to LOSE WEIGHT or a calorie SURPLUS to GAIN WEIGHT but nothing in life is black and white and the same can be said for calories. Calories are not the whole picture, but are of course an important element.

Calories are basically a unit of energy that are either ingested (Energy In) or utilised (Energy Out) but foods that have basically the same amount of calories may also have other macro-or micronutrients attached to them, which could cause reactions or interactions in the body that may have a positive or negative impact, even though they have the same unit of energy.

The most extreme example to give you is to compare the following two foods with the same number of calories. For this example, let's say we have 100 calories of both refined sugar and raw broccoli:

100 calories refined sugar

- Weight – 25 g

Macronutrients

- Protein – 0 g
- Fats – 0 g
- Carbohydrates – 25 g
- Sugars – 25 g
- Fibre – 0 g

Micronutrients

- Calcium (%) – 0.03
- Iron (%) – 0.07

We can see that aside from the total calories and carbohydrates from sugar, refined sugar is completely lacking in all other macro- and micronutrients, it is calorie dense but nutrient deficient, much like a lot of the junk food available these days.

100 calories raw broccoli

- Weight – 300 g

Macronutrients

- Protein – 8.4 g
- Fats – 0.4 g
- Carbohydrates – 19.9 g
- Fibre – 7.8 g

Micronutrients

- Vitamin A (%) – 37
- Vitamin C (%) – 446
- Calcium (%) – 14
- Iron (%) – 11

We can see that raw broccoli is by definition a nutrient-dense food; for the same amount of calories/energy there is 12 times the volume of food to eat, when compared with the refined sugar which is a calorie-dense food, 12 times less volume but with the same amount of calories/energy.

This is the best example of a calorie-dense food versus a nutrient-dense food, especially when looking at the fibre content of them both, sugar having 0 g of fibre and broccoli having 7.8 g of fibre, which is nearly a quarter of the daily recommended intake.

Both foods would react very differently within the body even though they have the same 'energy' value.

Due to the lack of other nutrients (especially fibre) and the large amount of carbohydrates/sugars, eating 100 calories of sugar would spike your blood sugar, giving you a quick spike and equally fast crash in energy, which could be dangerous in terms of blood sugar regulation for some, and would leave you feeling very hungry quite soon after eating it.

The broccoli on the other hand is a larger volume of food, 300 g vs 25 g, which would keep you full for quite a long period of time, especially due to the fibre content. It would also help you with immune health, energy, recovery and growth thanks to the protein and micronutrient contents. The broccoli does also contain 20 g of carbohydrates but thanks to the fibre, protein and lack of refined sugars it would not dangerously elevate blood sugar but would give you a slower release of energy.

It's Not an Exact Science

The important thing to remember is that calorie counting is not an exact science. There are always going to be slight variations in the calorie content of foods. You must also put trust in the labels that you're reading unless you weigh and calculate all of your own food.

But what calorie counting does give for you is a starting point, a place to begin your journey from. Just like with the setting of the Outcome Goal or destination for your journey, calorie counting sets you off from a specific place, it's then for you to regularly measure your progress along the way to stay on track ensuring that you reach your goal.

Just like any journey or writing of a book for instance, you must always have a beginning, middle and end. Calorie counting gives you these points to adjust and measure against.

I have used calorie counting myself very successfully when competing for fitness shows, dieting over a period of approximately 12 weeks. The pictures below logged my progression for my show prep for the WBFF Denmark Fitness Model show back in 2013, and through calculating my calorie intake, I was able to project what my target weight and body fat could be on a certain day and as you can see on April 1st I hit my predicted target.

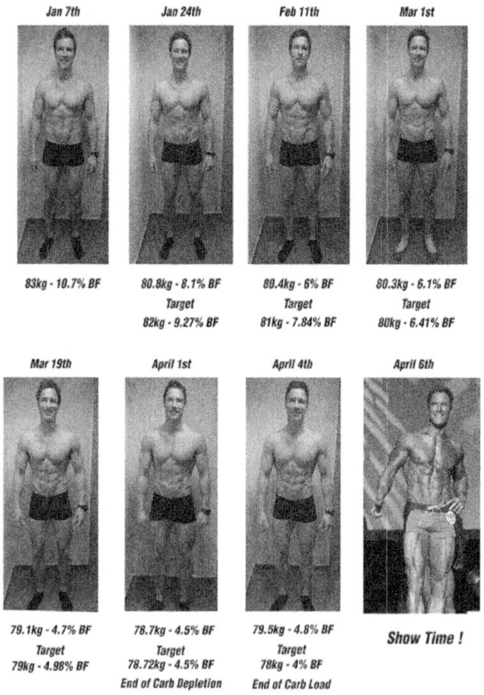

Calculating Calorie Intake

There are many more accurate equations and methods of calculating your calorie intake that consider other factors such as activity level, age, body type, etc. but as I said this isn't an exact science and have found the below calculation a very basic but effective method to get started. You can then monitor progression and adjust accordingly.

NOTE: To convert your bodyweight from kilos to pounds, just times your weight by 2.205.

- **Fat/Weight Loss** – Bodyweight (lbs) x 13
- **Maintenance** – Bodyweight (lbs) x 14
- **Muscle/Weight Gain** – Bodyweight (lbs) x 15

Real Life Doesn't Always Fit with Equations...

Weight Gain – I had a young male client about 65 kg who should have been gaining weight on a calorie surplus of 2,400 kcal per day but we took him to 3,000 kcal and he still struggled to gain weight.

Weight Loss – I had a female client of about 60 kg who we got up to 2,000 kcal per day and she was still losing weight.

This is why it's a great way to create a starting point but monitoring progression and adjusting regularly is essential, as everyone's body reacts differently to training and nutrition.

For instance, if you calculate your calorie intake for weight/fat loss and after one to two weeks you're not seeing any loss in weight then you would first increase your training volume and reassess after another week. If you still saw no progress then you would reduce your daily calorie intake by 100, then reassess again in one to two weeks and repeat the process.

Patience is key, always try to increase training volume first before lowering calories, drop too many calories too soon and you may start impairing your body's natural metabolic response to training and nutrition.

Likewise, if you calculate your calorie intake for muscle/weight gain and after one to two weeks you're not seeing any gain in weight then you would increase your calorie intake by 100 calories per day and then reassess again in one to two weeks.

Note: Making small adjustments and then monitoring how your body behaves will prevent either a rapid loss in weight – including muscle loss and a reduced metabolic rate, which we obviously want to avoid – or a rapid increase in weight which will most likely be made up of more body fat than lean muscle.

Self-Experiment

Sometimes you need to do some self-experimentation to really find out what works for you and your body, and this will change as your body does. Use my advice as a guide and initial starting point, then self-regulate and monitor your nutrition as you learn more about your body and what combinations of fuel it functions optimally on. Remember, throughout the process to...

MONITOR, ADJUST AND APPLY!

Simple and Sustainable

So calorie counting does work, there is no denying that. It gives you a more detailed approach to your energy balance and needs, which is justified when the goal is a much more extreme one and for a short period of time. But do you want to be counting calories at every meal for the rest of your life, locked into a rigid set of figures? is it a sustainable approach to nutrition and is it necessary for optimising health, body composition and performance?

I've come to realise that while food quantity is an important factor, food quality should take an equal if not higher priority in the equation.

If your focus is on eating as many diverse and nutrient-dense foods as opposed to calorie-dense foods then you will naturally eat less of the foods that can cause problematic health conditions and weight gain, while consuming more of the foods that will optimise your health and give you abundant energy.

The simpler we can keep our approach to training and nutrition the more sustainable your habits will become. If you have to integrate a complicated thought or action into your life every day, it becomes much harder to maintain consistency. And as we discussed in previous chapters, it's that consistency applied over a prolonged period of time which is critical to achieving any goal.

So, remember Plant Powered Principles number 3...

If it's not Simple, then it's not Sustainable.

PORTION CONTROLLING MADE SIMPLE

So, if we're not going to use calorie counting to measure our portions then what will we use? Remember the criteria is that it must be a Simple and Sustainable method of portion controlling.

Well there's a couple of methods we can use. The first method is with your hands as we are all blessed with limbs that are generally the same ratio to the size of our bodies. Big person equals big hands, smaller person equals smaller hands. Simple so far?

So, a very effective way to measure out your portions is by using your hands as guides.

A good rule of thumb, excuse the pun, would be to measure the different macronutrients using the following guide for a balanced meal:

Small Appetite

- **Proteins** – 1 cupped-hand sized portion
- **Carbohydrates** – 1 cupped-hand sized portion
- **Fats** – 1 thumb-sized portion (1 tbsp for oils)

Big Appetite

- **Proteins** – 2 cupped-hand sized portions
- **Carbohydrates** – 2 cupped-hand sized portions
- **Fats** – 2 thumb sized portions (2 tbsp for oils)

Then once you have portioned your main macronutrients

out, the rest of your meals should be made up of nutrient-dense vegetables and some fruit, eating as much as you like to increase the nutrient density. But generally for a single meal aim for:

- **Vegetables** – 2–3 cupped-hand sized portions
- **Fruit** – 1–2 cupped-hand sized portion(s)

With regards fruit, it is best to eat your fruit before a meal due to the faster rate of digestion and to consume lower carbohydrate fruit such as berries with a big meal, especially if you're already consuming a lot of starchier carbohydrates such as potatoes and grains.

Eating your quota of fruit after exercise is the perfect time, as it capitalises on your body's ability to utilise carbohydrates more effectively and helps to replenish liver glycogen first.

A Word on Berries

Not only are berries low in carbohydrates in the form of fruit sugar, they also provide you with a massive dose of disease-fighting antioxidants and other super nutrients to optimise your health. The purple-blue-red-orange spectrum is home to the most antioxidant-rich fruits.

One study showed you can increase the bioavailability of some berries, especially blueberries, by lightly steaming them. This is also the same for other plant foods such as spinach and tomatoes. I particularly enjoy gently cooking my berries in a pan until they break down and go all gooey; this makes for a delicious dessert topping on porridge, yoghurt, nuts, seeds, etc.

Use Your Plate

Another really simple way to look at the way you construct and portion control your meals is to use your plate, split into different sections relevant to each macronutrient.

We can use the plate effectively as a kind of pie chart to help us allocate the correct amounts of food for each meal, as with the diagram on page 194. This is an example of a nutritionally balanced plate of food, broken down into the following sections:

Vegetables 50%

A nutrient-dense and diverse range of vegetables are the priority for all our meals, making up 50% of the plate. This ensures that at every meal you're consuming a wide range of different coloured vegetables.

Protein 25%

We all know vegans have issues with protein (jokes) but seriously it is essential that we all focus on a good source of protein for immune health, energy, recovery and maintaining muscle mass whatever your goals are. This may come from beans, legumes, tofu, tempeh, seitan or a plant protein powder.

You will also pick up additional protein and amino acids from all other plant foods as well; the above examples are the more protein-dense plant foods.

Carbohydrates 15%

There is obviously carbohydrates in most plant foods and I will discuss carbohydrates and their definition more extensively in the next chapter; but for now a good rule of thumb for a balanced meal would be to include the starchier varieties of carbohydrates – such as grains, brown rice pastas, noodles, potatoes, sweet potatoes – and the higher carbohydrate root vegetables, such as parsnips, along with all fruit on 15% of your plate. This will give you plenty of energy but will prevent overeating, which we all know is so easy when it comes to cooking up a big batch of these starchier carbohydrates.

Fats 10%

Last but by no means least is the fat portion on our plate. Fats are an essential source of nutrients and energy, also necessary for the transportation of fat-soluble vitamins vital for our health. But fats are also very calorie dense – for every 1 g of fat you get 9 calories, as opposed to every 1 g of protein and carbohydrate for which you get 4 calories. With this in mind, you can see how easy they are to overconsume, due to the caloric density. Don't be afraid of fats though, they are essential, just don't do a 'Pooh Bear' and stick your fist into a jar of almond butter believing that it's 'healthier' for you than peanut butter.

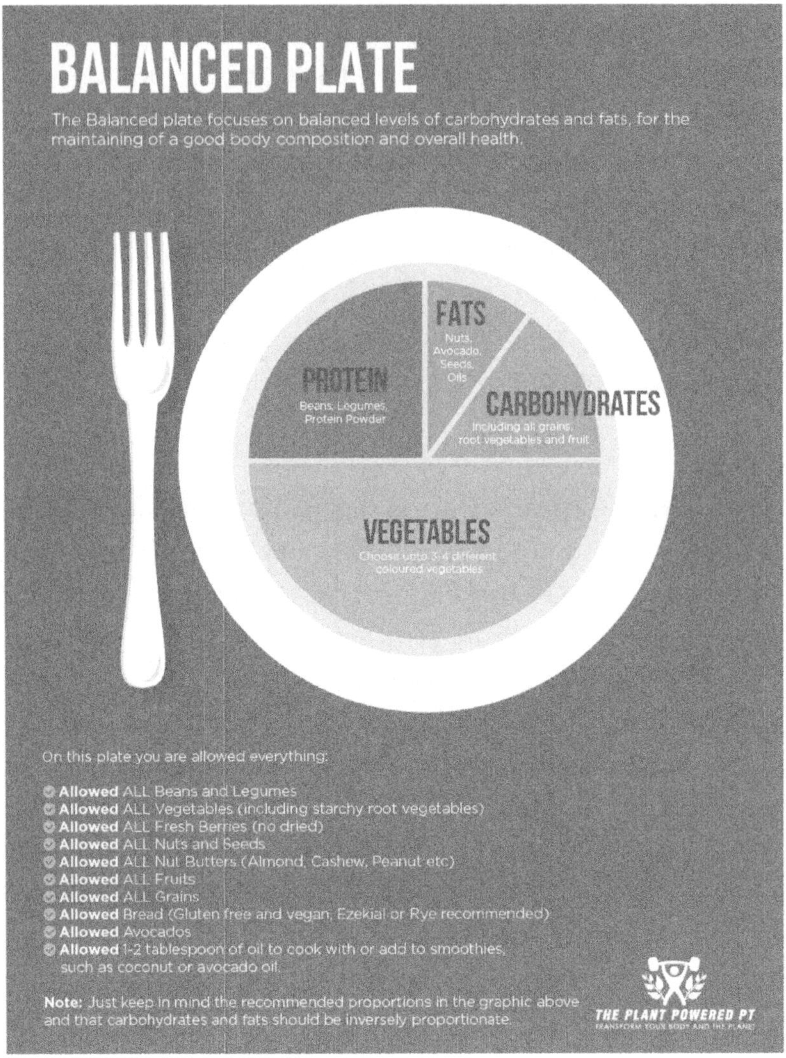

Plant Foods and their Macronutrients

You may well be a little confused now as to how you categorise plant foods into the different macronutrient categories of protein, carbohydrates and fats, as so many plant foods have a combination of all three.

As human beings we have 'bastardised' the notion of what food is made up of and have conveniently broken everything down into the neat labels of protein, carbs and fats. But nature is so much smarter than that and includes all the macro and micronutrients we need together in plants. Nature takes a synchronistic approach to everything, providing us with the right quantities we need and the right nutrients that work together.

I don't want us to get stuck in the weeds (excuse the pun) as we want to keep everything 'Simple and Sustainable' and use principles that are easy for us to apply, so it's important that we don't get too wrapped up in the details and overcomplicate matters. I generally categorise my plant foods in the appropriate macronutrient category depending on which macro is the most dominant in that food. For example:

Technically seeds such as hemp and chia are high in protein and a very good source of it for vegans. They also have a decent amount of carbohydrates in them, but they are most dominant in fats, so I would class them as a source of fat rather than protein or carbohydrates.

Many nuts also contain protein and carbohydrates along with a more dominant fat content, so when building a meal I would class these as a source of fat as well.

Beans actually have a higher amount of carbohydrates in them than protein, but I would still class these as a protein source on a plant-based diet, as finding totally isolated naturally occurring plant-based proteins is not possible.

Here is a Venn diagram I have made up to help give you an idea of how certain foods are broken down. This will help you to classify them in your mind.

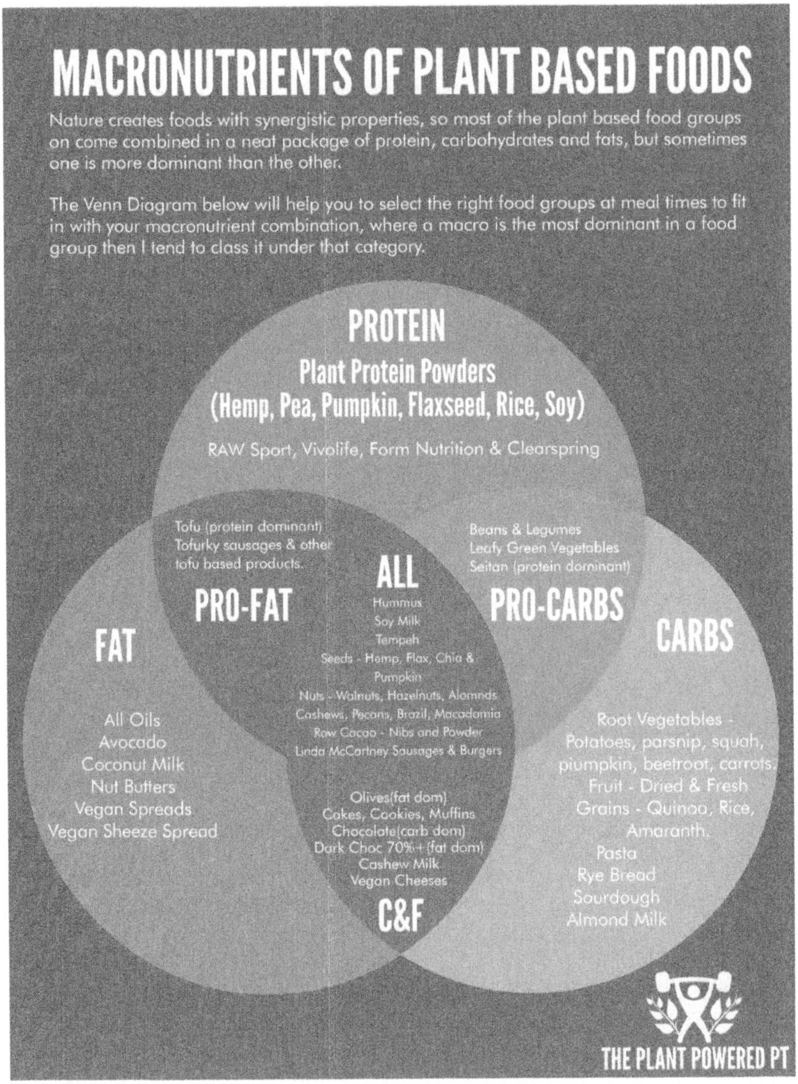

CHAPTER RECIPE

VEGAN COTTAGE PIE

Worried about missing out on that warm and comforting cottage pie during the winter months? Don't worry, we've got you covered. This is super easy to make and delicious, you won't miss a thing.

Servings: 2–3 hearty portions, depending on what else you serve with it. We usually serve this with peas, cabbage, broccoli and/or roasted carrots.

Ingredients:

- 4–5 big potatoes
- 4 portobello mushrooms
- 1 red onion diced
- 1 clove of garlic crushed or finely chopped
- 1 tbsp yeast flakes with added B12
- 1 pack/230 g of organic cooked lentils
- 2 tbsp apple cider vinegar
- 2 tbsp vegan Worcestershire sauce
- 2–3 tbsp vegan gravy powder
- Salt
- Pepper
- Olive oil

You will need:

- 1 pan for boiling potatoes
- 1 large frying pan with lid for cooking the mixture
- 1 large oven dish
- 1 chopping board

- 1 sharp knife

Cooking Method:

For the mashed potato topping:

1. Boil the potatoes, then mash with yeast flakes, salt, pepper and a few drops of olive oil.

For the filling:

1. Shred the portobello mushrooms and pan fry until the water has evaporated. Put aside in a bowl.
2. Pan fry one red onion and one clove of garlic until brown.
3. Then add the mushrooms and one pack of organic lentils, also adding the apple cider vinegar, vegan Worcestershire sauce, vegan gravy powder and add enough hot water to almost cover the mix. Season with salt and pepper but be careful not to overdo the salt due to the vegan gravy powder. Then simmer until the sauce thickens and liquid evaporates. **NOTE**: If you don't have vegan gravy powder just add a vegetable stock cube and thicken with a tablespoon of gluten-free flour, powdered oats or ground flaxseed.
4. Add the mixture to a dish and then the mashed potato and bake in an oven for 30 minutes at 200^{oC} or until the topping has browned.
5. Serve with the vegetables of your choice and a big dollop of wholegrain mustard.

Now that's Plant Power!

CHAPTER 15
CARBOHYDRATE CYCLING

Fats and carbohydrates should be inversely proportionate.

As discussed in earlier chapters regarding calories, we must always first make sure that you are in a caloric deficit or surplus depending on your goal (lose or gain), but to make the process much more efficient and for a more effective nutritional strategy we can work with the body's natural prioritisation of energy sources.

If fat is high in a meal then carbohydrates should be lower; if carbohydrates are high then fats should be lower.

This is an important rule to apply when improving body composition (the ratio of body fat to lean muscle) and one of the reasons many people – meat eater or plant eater – experience an inability to shift stubborn body fat.

It's thanks to eating meals that are both high in carbohydrate and fats together (like most junk foods) that the Western world is so plagued with dietary diseases. They are also made like this because it stimulates all our taste receptors.

Low-carb or a low-fat diet both work, because the other is not present.

For example, trail mix is a delicious and a much healthier snack than a Mars bar but you're eating fat-dense foods such as nuts and sugary carbohydrate-dense foods such as dried fruit together, providing an overabundance of two different forms of energy. Great if you're an endurance athlete or surviving in the wild and need all the calories you can find, but not so good if you're sitting at a desk all day gorging on a bag of trail mix.

Metabolic Priority

The body prioritises which fuels are burned first by their storage ability. The easier a fuel is to store, the lower down it goes on the list for immediate fuel use.

Metabolic or oxidative priority dictates that order:

- Alcohol
- Protein/amino acids
- Carbohydrate
- Fat

If the one above is present, that will take priority in terms of energy production, so in terms of eating a meal that is both high in carbohydrates and fat, the body will prioritise the burning of carbohydrates and store the fat, as fat is the easiest fuel source to store for the body to use later.

Therefore, for improving body composition, Fats and Carbohydrates Should Be Inversely Proportionate.

Note: This is also why a KETO diet is not actually a high-protein diet, as excessive protein and amino acids would be burned before fats, which is the objective. A real keto diet actually contains a fairly low amount of protein.

Defining Carbohydrates

It's all too easy to jump on the carb-hatred bandwagon these days but there really is no need. Like many things in life, it's not quite as black and white as good or bad; it's somewhere in the middle where the truth lies, as not all carbohydrates are created equal.

As soon as you mention carbohydrates, many people develop a cold sweat and start putting on weight just by imagining plates of refined carbohydrates such as pasta, bread, doughnuts and pastries.

But carbohydrates are found in many plant foods, ranging from high to low in fruit, starchy root vegetables such as sweet potato, potato, carrots, corn, parsnips, butternut squash, pumpkin, beetroot, etc. But they are of the 'wholefood' variety, meaning that they contain many other vitamins, minerals and nutrients that are lacking with the refined varieties of carbohydrates, that have isolated ingredients and removed the more nutrient-dense elements of the food, which we need to thrive.

A wholefood plant-based diet should focus on the carbohydrates that nature created such as fruit, starchy vegetables, and healthy grains, then you won't go far wrong and carbohydrates can be your friend rather than your enemy.

What is Carb Cycling?

Planned alteration of carbohydrate intake to prevent a fat loss plateau, maintain metabolism and workout performance.

Whenever you eat a diet that is restrictive on calories and carbohydrates, your body will automatically start to reduce energy expenditure and increase hunger. This is done through the reduction of the hormone leptin, which will in turn slow down your metabolic rate, thus slowing down fat-burning potential and attempt to increase energy intake to buffer stored energy for survival.

Body fat secretes leptin in the body, so the less body fat you have then the less stored energy you have to secrete the hormone. So as your body fat gets lower, so do the levels of leptin in the body.

Insulin increases leptin secretion in fat cells. As far as the body is concerned, if insulin is present in decent amounts then the body assumes that you have just eaten food and/or food is readily available in your environment.

The carbohydrate content of a diet also effects leptin levels independent of insulin. Protein also has the same effect but to a lesser degree and fat doesn't seem to have any effect.

To keep your body expending energy and burning body fat consistently we must stimulate the body to produce more leptin by periodically increasing carbohydrate and/or calorie intake.

Who does it work for?

- Carbohydrate cycling and leptin stimulation is most effective in the lean, moderately lean, and those carrying a slight excess in body fat.
- Anyone with 'stubborn' body fat, or those who are lean and have plateaued in their fat-loss efforts.
- If you've been eating a low-carbohydrate diet for a while but your energy is now lower and you're not feeling as good as when you started.

Who doesn't it work for?

Generally, people carrying excessive amounts of body fat will do much better initially on a lower carbohydrate approach full stop, until their body fat and weight is down to a more natural level and the body begins to need more encouragement for energy expenditure.

Using Your Plate for Carb Cycling

The images overleaf are examples of how you might use the plate template in terms of carbohydrate cycling. While maintaining the same ratio of vegetables (50%) and protein (25%) all we are doing is manipulating the levels of carbohydrates and fats during each meal.

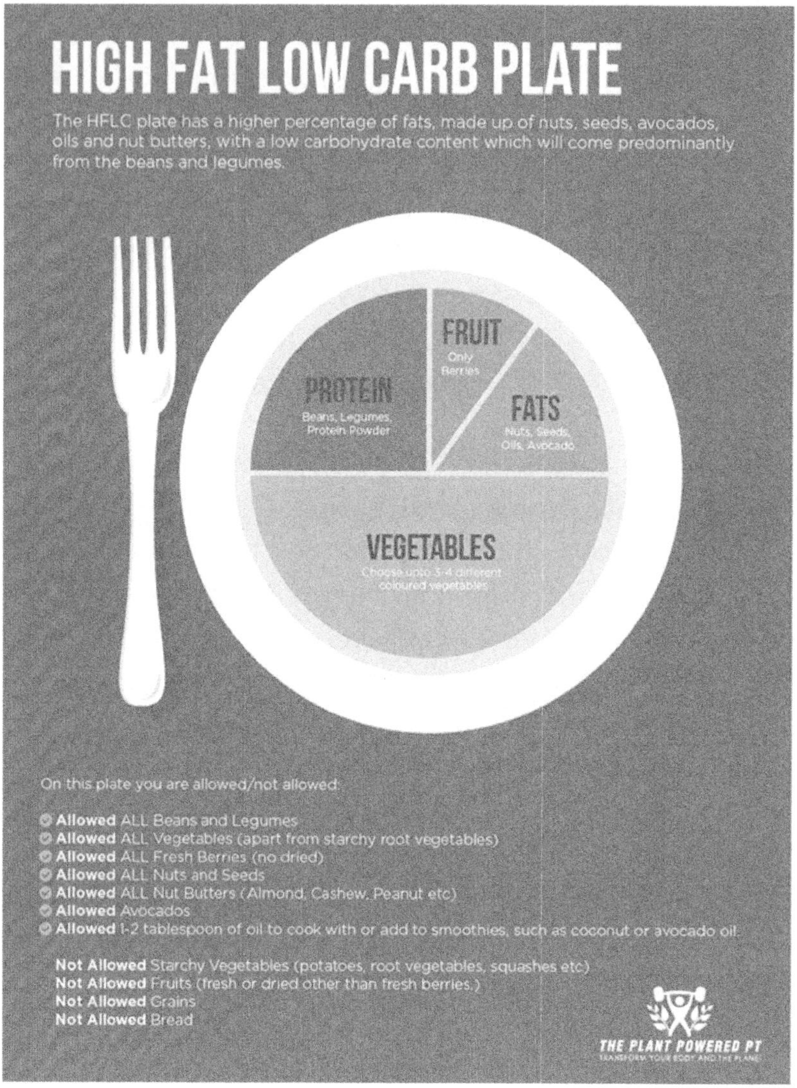

High-Fat Low-Carb Plate (HFLC)

This plate's focus is on a high-fat content to replace the calories/energy lost with the reduction in carbohydrates and allows for a source of fruit but only from berries, due to their lower carbohydrate content. Starchy and refined carbohydrates are off the menu here.

High-Carb Low-Fat (HCLF)

This plates focus is on a high-carbohydrate content allowing ALL the starchy carbohydrates back in (minimising refined foods where possible for optimal health). All fruit is allowed but fats are reduced to a minimal amount such as cooking with a small amount of oil or to lightly dress salads.

This is a very effective way of applying our 'Simple and Sustainable' approach to portion controlling, with a more advanced nutritional strategy, to help with improving body composition, health and performance.

Carb cycling though is not just for fat loss, it can also be used to support performance when increased energy production is needed. Basically focusing your carbohydrate intake on days that you are more active is a simple and effective way to use this strategy.

Carb cycling etc. is not needed for people looking just to lose a bit of weight or to be healthy. You should focus on a balanced approach to all macronutrients with food quality your main concern. But remember, if you want to lose weight, you must be consuming less energy than you are expending.

CHAPTER RECIPE

COURGETTI, EDAMAME, PEAS AND HOMEMADE PESTO

This is a quick, delicious, fresh, light and simple lower carbohydrate meal, and is also a great example of how you can turn a meal into a higher carbohydrate meal if required.

Just swap the courgetti out for a gluten-free, high-protein pasta, replace the pine nuts with 50 g tofu – the tofu when blended binds the pesto together as the pine nuts would but with less fat – and replace the extra virgin olive oil for more apple cider vinegar.

Servings: 1–2

Ingredients High Fat Low Carb (HFLC):

- 150 g edamame beans (prepared, tinned or frozen)
- 1 large courgette turned into courgetti noodles
- 100 g peas
- 2 tbsp of extra virgin olive oil
- 1 pack fresh basil
- 1 handful fresh pine nuts
- 1 tbsp apple cider vinegar
- 1 clove fresh garlic
- ½ fresh lemon
- Salt and black pepper

Ingredients High Carb Low Fat (HCLF):

- 150 g edamame beans (prepared, tinned or frozen)
- 100 g gluten-free spaghetti (brown rice is my favourite

alternative)
- 100 g peas
- 3 tbsp apple cider vinegar
- 1 pack fresh basil
- 50 g tofu
- 1 clove fresh garlic
- ½ a fresh lemon
- Salt and black pepper

You will need:
- 1 large frying pan with a lid
- 1 chopping board
- 1 sharp knife
- 1 serving bowl
- 1 large saucepan (to cook the pasta for the high-carb version)

Cooking Method HFLC (High Fat Low Carb):
1. Turn the courgette into noodles through a spiraliser and set to one side in a bowl.
2. To make the pesto add the basil, garlic, olive oil, apple cider vinegar, pine nuts, salt and black pepper to a small blender or food processor and blend until you have a smooth green consistency. Keep a few basil leaves for decoration.
3. In the large frying pan add the edamame beans and the peas together with a drop of water and replace the lid for a couple of minutes until they have just cooked.
4. Add the freshly made pesto to the beans and peas, stir through to release the flavours for a minute, then add the courgetti and replace the lid and cook until the courgetti has just softened. This will take 1–2 minutes.

5. Serve in a bowl, top with a couple of fresh basil leaves, a squeeze of fresh lemon juice and some freshly ground black pepper.

Cooking Method HCLF (High Carb Low Fat):

1. Bring a pan of water to the boil and add the spaghetti. It will take approximately 10 minutes.
2. To make the pesto add the basil, garlic, tofu, apple cider vinegar, salt and black pepper to a small blender or food processor and blend until you have a smooth green consistency. Keep a few basil leaves for decoration.
3. In the large frying pan add the edamame beans and the peas together with a drop of water and replace the lid for a couple of minutes until they have just cooked.
4. Add the freshly made pesto to the beans and peas, stir through to release the flavours for a minute, then add the cooked spaghetti and combine the ingredients.
5. Serve in a bowl, top with a couple of fresh basil leaves, a squeeze of fresh lemon juice and some freshly ground black pepper.

CHAPTER 16

EMBRACING YOUR BODY

"I have to be me, to be truly free."

One of the first and healthy acknowledgements to make when looking to transform your body is to understand your genetic limitations and advantages. It's great to be inspired when you look at the physique of another man or woman but always remember that although we are all generally anatomically the same, we all express different genetic variations in some shape or form, internally or externally, and the way one person's body builds muscle or has a specific shape may not be the same way that yours does or will.

This is not a defeatist attitude in any way, its time saving, as it prevents you wasting valuable energy and focus trying to look like someone else or be someone else. Instead it focuses your energy on embracing your own body, its perfectly individual shape and the advantages that it brings for you. Self-love, I've learnt, is so important in our lives, it gives us freedom to just be who we are.

This was a great lesson I learnt when competing in shows. At the beginning I would look enviously at other guys who had such thick, round muscles compared to mine, or a different shaped chest, but once I let go of the fact that we are all built differently genetically and that I had great abs, good forearms and shoulders of my own, I started competing against myself rather than against other people. My goal was always just to be the best version of myself, beating my previous physique. It then no longer mattered whether I came first or last, as long as I had improved myself. This mindset set me free.

BODY TYPES

There are generally three different distinct body types that we are all made up of. Usually we are a combination of two:

Ectomorph – Skinnier/longer limbed
Endomorph – Thicker set/wider frame
Mesomorph – Athletic and muscular

It's good to gain an understanding of which body types you're made up of, as this will help determine what kind of macronutrient ratios you thrive on for health, body composition and performance.

Usually people who are leaner naturally thrive much better on a diet that is higher in carbohydrates and lower in fat, due to the body's ability to assimilate carbohydrates more efficiently when it is in a much leaner state. This is thanks to more balanced blood sugar and insulin sensitivity.

Whereas people who are carrying more body fat will do much better on a diet that is higher in fat and lower in carbohydrates, until they have reduced their body fat to a level where they can process carbohydrates much more efficiently, as I discussed earlier in the section on carbohydrate cycling.

Below is a summary of the three general body types. Remember that we are generally not just one but a blend of two:

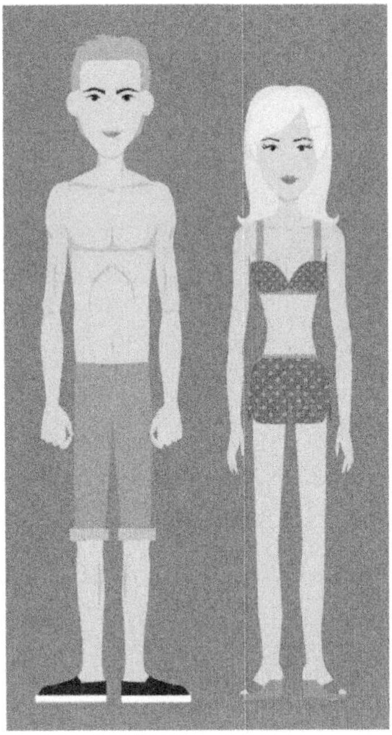

ECTOMORPH

- Naturally thinner build
- Longer limbed
- Low body fat
- Find it harder to put on weight
- Function better on a diet higher in carbohydrates and lower in fats.

Recommended Macro Split

- **Protein** – 20%
- **Carbohydrates** – 60%
- **Fats** – 20%

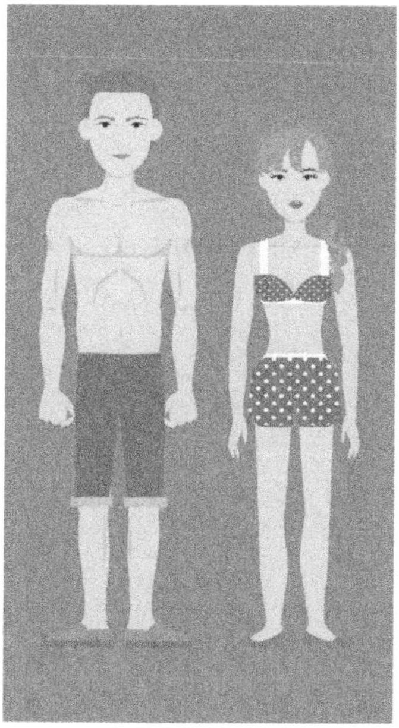

MESOMORPH

- Athletic and muscular
- Find it easier to maintain low body fat
- Find it easier to add and maintain muscle mass
- Function better on a diet that is a balance of both carbohydrates and fats

Recommended Macro Split

- **Protein** – 25%
- **Carbohydrates** – 45%
- **Fats** – 30%

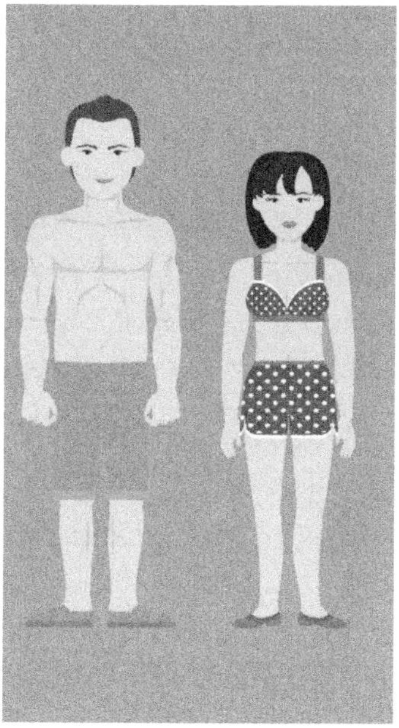

ENDOMORPH

- Naturally thicker build
- Wide around waist
- Higher body fat
- Find it harder to lose weight
- Function better on a diet higher in fats and lower in carbohydrates

Recommended Macro Split

- **Protein** – 30%
- **Carbohydrates** – 20%
- **Fats** – 50%

The above macronutrient ratios are general recommendations If you can't match the exact percentages, then try to keep the ratios of carbohydrates to fats inversely proportionate.

Hitting 25–30% protein on a planet-based diet may prove harder while keeping the other two macronutrients at their respective levels. You can always tweak the protein content of a meal by using specific high-protein plant-based foods to ensure you maintain the percentages of the other macronutrients:

Suggestions for Increasing Protein

- **Ectomorph** – Use beans or seitan as they are a protein source that is higher in carbohydrates.
- **Mesomorph** – Use beans as they are a protein source that is higher in carbohydrates, or tempeh as it contains a more favourable balance of fats to carbohydrates than tofu.
- **Endomorph** – Use tofu as it is a protein source that is higher in fat.

This is where plant protein powders can come in really handy to help boost the protein content in a diet, but to simplify things and avoid an overreliance on protein powder, step away from the exact figures and percentages above and use your plate to ensure if fats are high in a meal, then carbohydrates are low. You really can't go wrong with the plate templates that I've already outlined, if counting calories is not for you.

You only NEED more protein, if you NEED more protein! Your goals and activity level should guide you.

CHAPTER RECIPE

SOURDOUGH MUSHROOM STEAK TOASTIES

These open sourdough toasties were off the scale, especially after I topped them with mashed avo, caramelised red onions and then the sliced portobello mushroom steaks.

Basically, tamari and mushrooms are a winning combination in the flavour race!

This little mushroom adventure was inspired by the mushroom adventures of Derek and Chad Sarno and their Wicked *Healthy* cookbook.

Servings: 2 toasties, 1 each, 2 if you're famished!

Ingredients:

- 2 slices of sourdough bread
- 2 big portobello mushrooms
- 1 avocado
- 1 red onion finely sliced
- 1 clove of garlic crushed
- 1 tbsp apple cider vinegar
- 1 tbsp extra virgin olive oil
- 1 tbsp coconut, avocado or ground nut oil for cooking onions
- 1 tbsp yeast flakes with added B12
- 4 tbsp tamari
- Sprouts for topping (broccoli or alfa alfa are my favourites)

- Dash of tabasco
- Salt and pepper

You will need:

- 1 large frying pan
- 1 griddle pan
- 1 chopping board
- 1 sharp knife

Cooking Method:

1. Heat up a large frying pan (one with a lid preferably) and add 1 tbsp of coconut, avocado or ground nut oil, then add the finely sliced red onions. Add a little water and then place the lid back on the pan. Keep checking the onions, stirring and adding more water to stop them sticking and to help them breakdown.
2. While you're heating up a griddle pan, put the portobello mushrooms on a plate and coat each mushroom with 2 tbsp of the tamari, then drizzle with olive oil, salt, pepper and the crushed garlic, and massage it all into the mushrooms. Once the pan is hot, place the mushrooms on the griddle pan and then place another pan on top to press the mushrooms down. This will make them more steak-like, compact and full of flavour. Turn them every 2 minutes and replace the pan, turning for a maximum of twice per side.
3. Mash the avocado in a small bowl with salt, pepper, yeast flakes, apple cider vinegar, 1 tbsp olive oil, tabasco to taste and mix thoroughly.
4. Toast the 2 slices of sourdough.
5. To build the toastie, first spread the mashed avocado,

then add the mushrooms on top sliced thinly like steak, then top with the caramelised onions and the sprouts.

Sit somewhere quietly by yourself and immerse yourself in the flavours and textures.

CHAPTER 17

FIRING UP YOUR METABOLISM

"For 20% of the effort
you get 80% of the gain."
Pareto's Law

Now you've set your goals, understand the process, and have worked out your calorie and macronutrient needs, it's time we get physical and look at the quickest ways to get your metabolism fired up to work with the goal setting and nutrition principles we've discussed already.

Having a healthy metabolism to burn body fat is an essential part of this process. It requires us to work with our body rather than against it, stimulating it just enough so that it responds and works with us, rather than pushing it at 100% intensity day in day out that will lead to an unhealthy hormonal balance and slowing down of the metabolism.

Train Smarter not Harder

I think we are all guilty of believing in the concept that more or harder is better. Is it in our nature or a product of the world that we have grown up in, that makes us constantly push, push and push some more until we get there, or something breaks first? But life doesn't have to be that hard all the time.

Remember, earlier I mentioned that consistency and training frequency trumps intensity to realise improvements over a long period of time.

The ***Pareto principle*** *(also known as the* ***80/20 rule****, the* ***law of the vital few,*** *or the* ***principle of factor sparsity****) states that, for many events, roughly 80% of the effects come from 20% of the causes*

Management consultant Joseph M. Juran suggested the principle and named it after Italian economist Vilfredo Pareto, who noted the 80/20 connection while at the University of Lausanne in 1896, as published in his first paper, 'Cours d'économie politique'.

Essentially, Pareto showed that approximately 80% of the land in Italy was owned by 20% of the population; Pareto developed the principle by observing that about 20% of the peapods in his garden contained 80% of the peas.

Mathematically, the 80/20 rule is roughly followed by a power law distribution (also known as a Pareto distribution) for a particular set of parameters, and many natural phenomena have been shown empirically to exhibit such a distribution." Courtesy of Wikipedia

The Pareto principle has been applied to training as well, where roughly 20% of the exercises and habits have 80% of the impact and the trainee should focus less on exercise variety.

"I fear not the man who has practised 10,000 kicks once, but I fear the man who has practised one kick 10,000 times."

Bruce Lee

We can also apply the principle to HIIT and other forms of training in terms of time spent exercising. You need to let go of the widely thought ideal relating to:

More Time spent exercising = Greater Results

More does not always equal more results and in fact if you keep following that principle then you'll most likely burn out, regress and lose all the hard work you've put in.

Why work harder when you can work smarter and achieve the same results or better?

Don't get me wrong, if you don't work hard then no exercise programme will work for you, but it's about doing what's effective.

High-Intensity Interval Training

If we refer to Energy Balance, specifically Energy Out and exercise, as one of the five metabolic components, then of course we know any form of exercise or activity is going to stimulate a positive response to your energy expenditure.

But to stimulate your metabolism beyond the workout, we can employ two effective methods of training that will stimulate the metabolism to work harder and expend more energy.

EPOC – Excess Post-exercise Oxygen Consumption

Also known as creating an **Oxygen Debt**, this is achieved when the intensity of an exercise out-paces oxygen consumption, using commonly known strategies such as **HIIT (High-Intensity Interval Training)** will achieve this **Oxygen Debt**.

This oxygen 'debt' must be paid back once the level of activity again matches oxygen consumption. Therefore, oxygen consumption can be elevated for up to 36 hours post-activity depending on the duration and level of intensity. The three main reasons are to metabolise nutrients, replenish energy stores and reload oxygen stores in the muscles and blood.

Other factors that can contribute to the **EPOC** effect is increased body temperature post exercise, increased activity of the respiratory system and increased levels of metabolism-boosting hormones.

HIIT sessions aimed at metabolic improvements should be hard, short and fast – aim for a session anywhere between 5–15 minutes. If you're tempted to go 20–30 minutes you're not working hard enough or maybe creating unneeded additional stress on the body, moving away from that magical 20/80 law.

Lactic Acid

Lactic acid is a by-product of energy production (**ATP**) in your cells from the glycolytic energy system (utilising oxygen and glucose), during activities of around 10–12 seconds up to 2 minutes.

When your body is producing more **lactic acid** than your blood can remove, you experience that 'lovely' burning sensation in the targeted area. This is known as your **anaerobic** or **lactic** threshold.

Note: It is not the 'lactic acid' that creates the burning sensation; it is the splitting of the lactic acid into a lactate ion and hydrogen ion which lowers the pH of the blood to a more acidic level.

Lactic acid has a very beneficial effect on the production of hormones in the body, in that it stimulates the body to release **growth hormone** which in turn stimulates the breakdown of fat.

Top Tip: Increase lactic acid production by slowing down the tempo of your weightlifting, especially during the eccentric part of a movement (lowering), increasing the time under tension (TUT) on the targeted muscles.

Note: The amount of **growth hormone** released during intensive exercise can be up to nine times the level of normal **GH** output.

Long-Slow Duration Cardio (LSD)

Now, while the first two training strategies stimulate your body to release fat stores and elevate metabolic rate and energy expenditure post-exercise, they don't burn fat during the activity, due to the speed and intensity that energy needs to be produced.

Therefore, an effective fat-burning strategy would be to also use long-slow and low-intensity cardiovascular sessions after a HIIT session, to tap into the 'oxidative system', which uses oxygen and fat for energy supply.

This will also improve your 'aerobic' fitness level which will carry over and help in recovery during 'anaerobic' training sessions.

Warning: High-Intensity Interval Training should only be performed by those with a good base level of cardiovascular fitness, strength and body awareness. Otherwise you may fall prey to injury and will not reap the benefits, so increase intensity slowly.

NOTE: While Long-Slow Duration Cardio (LSD) may burn more calories and fat during the activity, it does not have such a direct effect on metabolism as the high-intensity anaerobic training does.

The Metabolic Rules

So, to summarise this chapter and to make sure you're headed for metabolic mastery, it is essential that we don't see ourselves separate from our body but instead work as a team with our body, stimulating it just enough so that we can benefit from its clever engineering.

Here's some important rules to remember for metabolic mastery:

- Train and Eat **Smarter** NOT **Harder**
- Be in a caloric **DEFICIT** or **SURPLUS** depending on your goal.

- Use **Carbohydrate Cycling** when applicable.
- Perform short but intense **High-Intensity Interval Training (HIIT)** workouts
- Increase **Lactic Acid** and slow down your weightlifting to increase the muscles **Time Under Tension (TUT)**
- **Sleep** and **Rest** thoroughly between workouts to maintain hormonal balance and a healthy metabolism.

CHAPTER RECIPE

JACKFRUIT RAGU WITH RIGATONI PASTA

Words can't describe the depth of flavour and mouth-drooling effects of this dish.

Part of the magic in this recipe was that we used vegan pesto and pasta made by www.seggiano.com, a super authentic Italian company, who's familiarity with Italian rural culture and their passion for excellent food enables partnership with the best artisan food producers of Italy. This of course gives your dishes a distinct Italian flavour.

If you wanted a higher protein content then you could substitute the jackfruit for non-GMO organic soy flakes, cooking the soy flakes for a long period of time in the ragu so it will absorb the flavours and give the dish a really meaty texture.

Servings: 2

Ingredients:

- 1 tin organic chopped tomatoes
- 1 tin jackfruit
- 1 onion sliced
- 1 clove garlic finely chopped
- Seggiano vegan tomato pesto
- Seggiano rigatoni pasta
- Cashews
- Yeast flakes

- Salt and pepper

You will need:
- 1 large saucepan
- 1 chopping board
- 1 sharp knife

Cooking Method:
1. Sauté the onion and garlic in a pan with a little olive oil and water to help soften and place a lid on the pan.
2. Then add the jackfruit to the pan and break it up as much as possible. Add a bit more water and place the lid back on the pan for a minute or two.
3. Then add the pesto and chopped tomatoes and place the lid back on with a little more water to prevent it all sticking and to increase the volume of sauce if needed.
4. Leave to simmer on a low heat for 30–60 minutes depending how long you have. The longer the better as the jackfruit will soften, break down and absorb all the flavours.
5. Serve with rigatoni pasta and top with cashew parmesan (blend cashews with yeast flakes and salt until fine).

CHAPTER 18

BUILDING MUSCLE

"Insanity is doing the same thing over and over again but expecting different results."
Albert Einstein

Let's start this chapter off by saying that there is absolutely no difference in the physiological mechanisms involved with building muscle on a plant-based vegan diet than there is with a meat-based diet. There may be a greater number of certain amino acids available on a meat-based diet that increase muscle growth, namely leucine, but this same amino acid may also have a negative impact on ageing, longevity and the growth of tumours, so what you gain on one hand you may lose on another.

Vegans and meat eaters still have the same muscles and mechanisms for muscle growth, they don't have to train differently, and they still need to follow the same training rules.

- Apply a progressively increasing overload of stimulation to the muscles.
- Rest and recover, allowing for adaptation to the environmental stimuli.

Muscular Hypertrophy

Hypertrophy is the technical term for *'an increase in size of skeletal muscle'* of which there are two different types:

Sarcoplasmic Hypertrophy

Is experienced through lighter loads and higher reps and is the increase in volume of sarcoplasmic fluid between muscle fibres, making trainees bigger but not necessarily stronger.

Myofibrillar Hypertrophy

Is experienced through strength training using heavier loads and more neuromuscular adaptation. This increases the number of actin and myosin fibres within the muscle making the trainee stronger but not necessarily bigger.

This is the kind of muscle growth and strength training athletes perform if taking part in sports that require weight classes, as this kind of hypertrophy increases 'relative strength' in relation to your body weight.

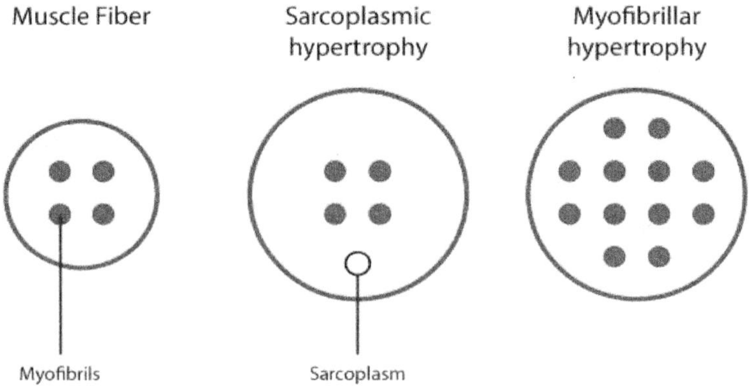

Lean muscle is what gives our bodies that desirable athletic look. Without the muscle, there would be no shape to our bodies. It's not that adding muscle can make us look bulky but excessive body fat sitting on top of the muscle can do this.

The term 'muscle building' can conjure up images of huge bodybuilders in people's minds but these are extreme bodies that the average person will never be able to build. However, we all need to focus on building lean muscle to help with body composition (muscle to fat ratio), performance (power, strength and movement) and health (metabolism), and should not be so afraid of the term 'bodybuilding', because we are all trying to build our bodies in some shape or form, striving for physical improvements that make our bodies more enjoyable for us to use and live in.

Here are three of the rules we need to focus on when building muscle:

- **Weight Training**
  Picking up and putting down progressively heavier objects/weights is essentially what we need to do if we want to start stimulating our body to respond. It's not just for the young; as we get older, lifting heavy weights (relative to your individual strength) will benefit us in terms of at least maintaining muscle mass, allowing us to function and move well into our later years and it will also have the added benefit of increasing bone density, which gets more important as we age.

- **Multi-Joint Exercises (Compound)**

These exercises give us the best bang for our buck in terms of muscular stimulation due to the amount of muscle being used to perform a movement, surrounding multiple joints. The stimulation of more muscle fibre also leads to increased metabolic effects, great for losing body fat. Example exercises would be bench press, chin-ups, deadlifts and squats.

- **Progressive Overload**

'If you do the same thing you've always done, then you'll get the same thing you've always got.'

This is another way of writing the Einstein quote that I started the chapter off with. It's an important lesson to learn in life but is an essential lesson to learn for building muscle.

Adding muscle to the human body is metabolically expensive. It takes much energy and valuable resources to add and maintain new muscle, therefore if you don't give your body the constant stimulation it needs for adaptation to take place, then it won't, and you will gradually lose it. This is known as 'atrophy', the opposite to 'hypertrophy'.

The body's main goal is survival while expending the least amount of energy. Once you understand this then it will make your muscle-building efforts much clearer, essentially you need to...

Get Comfortable Feeling Uncomfortable.

VEGAN MYTH BUSTING
STOP WORRYING ABOUT PROTEIN

And start worrying about your fibre intake, animal welfare and the environment.

But where do you get your protein from?

This has been the most commonly asked question posed to vegans for a long time although it is beginning to change as people become more vegucated.

The funny thing is no one cares about your protein intake until you tell them your vegan and then everyone turns into a nutritionist, but they forget to enquire as to whether you're also getting enough of the other 24-plus essential vitamins and minerals needed to function optimally as a human being. No one ever seems concerned about my zinc levels or whether I'm getting enough iodine, it's always protein, and that is thanks to clever marketing and our obsession with it.

The reality is that in the Western world we are not and are never likely to be protein-deficient. We overconsume animal protein in Western countries and have now added additional protein into nearly every form of food group we can imagine, not so much for the added nutritional benefit but more for marketing and sales, as protein has become the buzzword and the cure-all macronutrient. Many people are deficient in other nutrients (as we spoke about in chapter 13) rather than protein-deficient, plant based or not.

Saying all that, protein is of course essential but no more so than other essential nutrients and your protein intake should always be governed by your goals and activity levels.

Amino Acids

Amino acids are what make up 'protein' as we know it. These are grouped into two types: non-essential and essential amino acids that the body derives from protein, to use them for growth, repair, energy production and many other functions within the cells.

Non-Essential Amino Acids – These are synthesised by the body and readily available.

Essential Amino Acids – Are a group of nine amino acids that can't be synthesised by the body therefore must be obtained through diet. They are:

- Histidine
- Isoleucine
- Leucine
- Methionine
- Phenylalanine
- Threonine
- Tryptophan
- Valine
- Lysine

Animal-derived protein is considered a high-quality source of protein as it contains large quantities of all nine of the essential amino acids. It was once thought that plant protein sources were 'incomplete' and missed some of the essential amino acids, and that you would need to combine different foods to obtain the correct number of amino acids. This myth has now been dispelled. All the essential amino acids can be obtained from plant-based sources, but there are some amino acids that occur in lower numbers.

Protein is found in all plant foods. For example, the percentage of calories coming from protein in black beans is 24%, broccoli 32% and spinach 30%. Even fruits like peaches, avocados, strawberries and oranges derive approximately 5–9% of their calories from protein.

All amino acids can be obtained from plants, in just the right quantities that nature intended. It's important to remember the following statement for perspective...

"All essential amino acids originate from plants. Either you eat the plant, or you eat the animal that ate the plant. Either way, the essential amino acids came from the plant."
From Plant-Based Nutrition by Julieanna Hever, Raymond J. Cronise

---

So next time a meat eater asks you where you get your protein from, you can answer...

"The same place the animals you eat gets there's!"

Protein – or what we should more correctly refer to as amino acids – are all available from plant-based food sources. There's no need to combine but there is a need to eat a nutrient-diverse diet which will ensure that you get enough of those essential amino acids, without needing to supplement or to overly worry about it.

Your body is very clever at 'pooling' amino acids, removing the need to worry about food combining. These free amino acids are present throughout the body, in cells, blood, and the extracellular fluids. This pool is supplied by three sources:

- The breakdown of proteins in the body.
- Dietary intake of amino acids.
- Synthesis of non-essential amino acids through the metabolism.

It's obviously essential to make sure your diet is nutrient diverse and that you are regularly eating different sources of protein to ensure you have a wide range of these amino acids at your disposal.

We've been sold a myth surrounding the lack of protein in our diets, where it should come from and the amount we actually need. This is one of the main reasons that I wrote this book, to help dispel this protein myth. There's been a surge in popularity to build a beautiful body, increasing the need for lean muscle, a higher protein diet and until more recently a meat-based diet was pushed as the best way to get this protein and here we are.

What Else is in Your Protein?

Firstly, it's important for us to recognise the effect increased stress levels and out-of-control stress hormones are having on our health in society. We know that too many stress hormones lead to chronic disease conditions in humans and which led to my own problems and digestive surgery, so wouldn't stressed animals also secrete stress hormones into their bodies and flesh?

Imagine you're a cow or a pig and you are first transported for several hours in a truck to the slaughterhouse with very little light and even less room to move. Then you are lined up in a queue for slaughter, there's no way back and all you can hear ahead of you are the screams from your brothers and sisters. Can you even imagine the level of fear that you would be feeling? That fear translates biologically into the release of huge amounts of stress hormones, it's fight or flight time. After death, where do all those hormones end up – in your flesh.

Now we can probably guess that every animal entering a slaughterhouse that stinks of death is going to be going through a very traumatic experience. They know, they are sentient beings, and whether your meat has been fed grass or grain it matters not, they will all end up in the same slaughterhouse going through the same traumatic end-of-life process much sooner than their natural lifespan.

So now that meat is saturated in stress hormones, it's butchered up and goes to the supermarket. You buy, cook and ingest that stressed meat containing the stress hormones and now they are in your body. Remember, hormones are basically chemical signallers for your body, and these chemical signals could now be playing havoc in your body, maybe even causing stress, depression and anxiety within you.

Stress

I don't have a study to back this up and the next paragraph is based purely on my logic, observation and philosophical thinking.

We know that farmers do not actually want stressed animals before slaughter because of the effect it has on the meat quality. This is due to the release of cortisol and adrenaline before death which reduces the amount of glycogen in the muscle, which is converted into lactic acid. So, the more lactic acid the better quality, colour, tenderness of the meat and end-market product. Stress is bad for business, but can it be avoided in such horrific situations?

So that obviously means that animals lovingly reared and cared for living on free-range, grass-fed farms produce a better quality of meat than their unfortunate highly stressed cousins in factory farms, but they all end up at the same stressful slaughterhouses.

Another good reason to adopt my first Plant Powered Principle of 'Reducing Trauma and Suffering.'

Antibiotics

On factory farms, due to the volume of livestock being produced and the limited space, there is an obvious increase in the potential for disease and therefore an increase in the use of antibiotics to prevent this.

In the United States, approximately 80% of all antibiotics sold are used in animal agriculture and the WHO (Worldwide Health Organization) sees this as an increasing threat to global health.

December 2020: At the time of editing this manuscript we are currently locked into the Covid-19 pandemic which has shut down the global economy effecting billions of people. It is uncertain whether this came from animals in a wet market or a laboratory setting but it is yet another global disease that was given birth in an unnatural environment from the abuse of animals by humans, just like with Bird and Swine Flu.

We must start admitting that the mistreatment of animals in this way, is bad for our health as well as the animals.

Remember Plant Powered Principle number 1...

'Reduce Trauma and Suffering'

Hormones

In non-organic farming there are also other man-made growth hormones used in cattle such as trenbolone, zeranol and melengestrol acetate. These hormones are ingested by anyone who eats non-organic meats and the argument centres around the effect they may have on the human reproductive hormones and cycles.

Some populations face a much higher health risk, such as women who are pregnant and breast feeding. The dilemma lies in choosing a meal high in iron and animal protein vs the scare of ingesting and feeding hormones from the meat to their unborn child. And if we know that you can get plenty of iron and protein on a plant-based diet, why would you even take that risk?

Early onset of puberty, increasing incidence of twin births and reproductive problems have all been blamed on the hormones in meat. It has also been suggested that these growth hormones are linked to cancers, such as breast and uterine cancer, and developmental problems in children.

Great we'll just buy grass-fed and free-range then!

OK, well that's good for you if you are in the small percentage of the global population that can afford it, whereas the large majority must select more affordable and mass-produced meat.

Increase Population and Protein Demand

The trouble is that the human population on the planet is growing faster and faster, along with the demand for meat. This means that we end up with a scenario of less space for humans, but also needing to house more animals to satisfy the demand for meat, thus worse living conditions, more disease and poorer quality, potentially contaminated meat that is entering our food chain. We just won't have the space to feed the whole world with grass-fed and free-range meat, it is the luxury of the few that can afford it, rather than the mass population. We ALL need to start considering the effect our choices have on the rest of the planet.

If we can get all the protein/amino acids we need from plants, then isn't it time we stopped creating all these other damaging health and environmental issues for ourselves to satisfy our taste buds? The solution is right in front of us.

Fibre

No one in the Western world is protein deficient, but many people in the Western world are deficient in fibre.

With meat you're getting saturated fat, cholesterol and in non-organic meat potentially damaging toxins and hormones as mentioned above. But what aren't you getting with animal products?

Fibre, absolutely zero fibre comes from meat and dairy.

With plants, your amino acids are also coming with an abundance of vitamins, minerals, phytonutrients, antioxidants and fibre (soluble, insoluble and resistant starch), no external cholesterol or saturated fat, unless you gorge on the flesh of coconuts but then you'll also be getting a dose of fibre, carbohydrates, protein and minerals.

Fibre helps to balance blood sugar, slow down glucose metabolism, increases fullness, cleans out the digestive system and helps to feed your gut bacteria.

Of course, you can be a healthy non-vegan and an unhealthy vegan but while ensuring our individual health is important, we should ALL also have one eye on the effects that our food choices make on our environment and of course the animals that are turned into commodities for consumption.

The key is to ensure that your vegan diet is focused on a whole plant foods approach, reducing or eliminating as much as possible the refined man-made products that are so readily available but are nutrient deficient.

If you focus on the Double Ds that I spoke about earlier, nutrient density and diversity by eating the rainbow, you'll get all the nutrients, including the essential amino acids that you need to function optimally and have nothing to worry about.

In nature and the plant kingdom, macro or micronutrients just don't exist in isolation. They co-exist with each other, working together synergistically to provide exactly what you need. It's only when humans get in the way and decide that a specific nutrient can fix our problems, we strip all the other goodness away believing that more equals better and then we lose the magic of wholefood.

No one cares about your protein intake,
until they find out you're vegan.

Daily Intake

For most people wishing to live a healthy life, then 0.8–1 g of protein per kilo of bodyweight (per day) is plenty to achieve this.

The groups of people that require more protein are those that are physically active and looking to improve performance such as athletes, bodybuilders, etc. As the need for tissue growth, repair and recovery go up, then so do the protein requirements.

For these groups of people, 1.5–2 g per kilo of bodyweight should be an approximate target per day to aim for, leaning towards the higher end if muscle growth is your goal.

Building Muscle vs Slowing Ageing

The flipside to all this protein/amino acid talk is the effects that a specific amino acid and anabolic pathway (muscle growth mechanism in the body) combination has on the body to both help with building muscle but also increase ageing.

Leucine is the amino acid and mTOR is the pathway. When the amino acid leucine is in abundance it activates the pathway mTOR and increases muscle-building potential. Fantastic, I hear you say. Not so fast.

Studies have also shown that by reducing protein it suppresses both TOR and IGF-1, the two pathways thought responsible for the dramatic longevity and health benefits of caloric restriction. TOR plays a key role in development and ageing and has been implicated in disorders such as cancer, cardiovascular disease, obesity and diabetes.

Leucine has the greatest effect on these pathways and is found in large quantities in animal protein but is much lower in plant protein.

So, this is one perfect example of where having less of certain amino acids could well benefit your health and why getting your protein and amino acids from plants could benefit your life and health span over a meat-based diet.

More does not always equal better.

CHAPTER RECIPE

PLANT PROTEIN PANCAKES

This is the perfect lazy Sunday morning breakfast, packed full of flavour and of course plant protein for your muscle-building efforts.

Servings: 1 serving of 4 decent-sized pancakes

Ingredients:

- 150 ml non-dairy milk
- 50 g porridge oats
- 30 g plant protein powder (vanilla or unflavoured is best)
- 1 banana
- 1 tsp cinnamon
- 1 tsp baking powder

Suggested Toppings

blueberries, chopped nuts, seeds, soy or oat cream

You will need:

- 1 blender or food processor
- 1 non-stick frying pan or pancake maker
- 1 spatula

Cooking Method:

1. Preheat a non-stick pan on a medium heat.
2. Place all ingredients in a high-powered blender or food processor until smooth. If the batter looks too thick, just add a little more milk.
3. Pour the required amount of the batter into the pan.

Cook for 1–2 minutes and flip them with a spatula when bubbles have formed on the surface and the edges are slightly dry.

4. Cook until browned on the other side.

Top with blueberries, chopped nuts, seeds and some soy or oat cream to add extra flavour, texture and calories.

CHAPTER 19

PLANT-POWERED PERFORMANCE

"Performance is the best way
to shut people up."
Marcus Lemonis

One of the biggest concerns for many people making the switch from a meat-based diet to a plant-based one is whether it will affect their performance in the gym, sport and life. I'm here to tell you that it probably will, but for the better.

Do Vegans Workout Differently?

This was a question I was asked for *Women's Health UK* back in 2017. Here's how I answered, and this is also a good recap of some of the topics we have covered so far:

Q: If you're vegan, what are the main things you should do differently to non-vegans to ensure you're still working out effectively?

A: Nothing is the short and concise answer. Eating a plant-based diet doesn't mean you should have to or need to change the way you're working out in anyway. The same rules, 'Consistency and Commitment', still apply. You may even feel that your recovery in-between workouts improves.

Q: What do you need to make sure you're getting from alternative sources if you're exercising and not able to fuel up with animal protein etc?

A: The most important thing to ensure is a nutrient-dense and diverse diet, 'eating the rainbow' will ensure you optimise your nutrient intake. There's plenty of protein (amino acids) available from plant foods, and by ensuring you eat a diverse range of different coloured whole plant foods each day, you will support your training and nutrition needs.

Q: What are the best plant-based proteins and why are they particularly good if you're vegan?

A: Beans, legumes, nuts, chia, hemp seeds, tofu, tempeh (non-GMO), seitan (if you're not gluten intolerant) and plant protein powders are some of the best plant protein sources.

Q: How can you get energy pre-workout or refuel post-workout if you're vegan?

A: No different to that of a meat eater. Eating a good meal about two hours before or a nutrient-dense smoothie an hour before will set you up and energise you for your workout. Additional caffeine or cacao also works wonders. Sometimes I like some dark chocolate and a black coffee before training. The same applies post-workout, refuelling with either a nutrient-dense, protein-rich meal or similar nutrient-packed smoothie with bananas, berries, spinach and a scoop of plant protein powder for example.

Q: What are the best protein powders for vegans? Why are they specifically good?

A: Most plant protein powders are made from hemp, pea and rice protein, or they are a blend of the three, which gives the product a superior amino acid profile rather than if you just used one source.

Q: If you're vegan, how do you know if you're not fuelling yourself properly and overtraining?
A: Just the same as if you're a non-vegan. Watch out for overall fatigue, irritability, poor sleep, appetite loss and loss of libido.

The bottom line is that going vegan doesn't change the way you should approach exercise and training; you still need to fuel your body adequately for the task in hand or to recover afterwards. Also training frequency over training intensity wins in the long run, so rein in the intensity each session and you'll be able to train more frequently with less fatigue.

Nutrient density and diversity is a motto plant eaters and meat eaters alike would do well to focus on to optimise their health and performance.

The Game Changers

You must've seen *The Game Changers* by now? The movie documentary came out in 2019 and charts the success of many vegan athletes around the world participating in multiple disciplines such as strongman, Olympic lifting, sprinting, bodybuilding, ultra-marathon and many more.

It has some big names backing the production, such as James Cameron, Arnold Schwarzenegger, Jackie Chan, Lewis Hamilton and Novak Djokovic.

If you needed some hard evidence that your athletic

performance can thrive on a plant-based diet, then that documentary shows it in spades.

If anyone needs to be eating the best diet possible to enhance their physical body's performance, then it's a professional athlete. Their body is not just their vehicle but their livelihood, it needs to function at its optimal level if they have any chance of competing at a high level to win competitions and medals.

So, if it's good enough for an elite athlete it should be good enough for the average guy and girl who trains occasionally and has lower requirements for performance and recovery than an elite athlete.

How Can Plant Power Help My Performance?

The following plant-powered benefits can be experienced by anyone looking to perform better in their life, these aren't just reserved for just elite athletes.

Recovery of Champions

Thanks to the antioxidant content of plant foods, they can help remove inflammatory toxins from our blood such as 'free radicals', waste molecules that are produced during periods of high-intensity activity called 'oxidative stress' and that can lead to inflammation and a reduction of performance.

Thanks to this, plant foods have an anti-inflammatory effect on the body as opposed to many animal-based foods that can be pro-inflammatory.

The recovery potential of a plant-based diet is the main reason so many elite athletes are making the transition.

The Ideal Fuel Source

Carbohydrates are the optimal fuel source for our bodies, as we can store an adequate amount of it as glycogen in our liver and muscles, plus our bodies can convert it quickly from glucose into energy to fuel our activities.

As discussed earlier, though we should be looking to get our carbohydrate intake from unrefined wholefood sources like those found in oats, sweet potatoes, root vegetables and fruit.

Blood Flow Improvements

A plant-based diet has been shown to reduce blood thickness while also improving the flexibility and function of the lining in our heart and blood vessels.

The nitrates found in plant foods, improve the dilation of blood vessels increasing blood flow and the delivery of oxygen around the body.

Improved Muscular Efficiency

These blood flow improvements will also improve the oxygenation of tissues, providing much needed oxygen to cells helping to optimise muscular contractions.

My Own Performance

As I talked about in Part 1, I initially lost 4 kg in my early days as a vegan. Even though I felt I was eating a good diet, it was a change that my body needed time to climatise and adapt to. I'm also missing a vital digestive organ which does play a big part in my nutrient absorption and thus water/ weight loss.

This drastic loss in weight does not occur for most people. Even though it did in me, I knew that, once I connected to the negative effects of animal agriculture, I was going to make it work for me.

The juice was worth the squeeze.

I now sit comfortably at the same weight I was before I went vegan. I've lost body fat, added muscle and manipulated the carbohydrates and fats in my diet in the same way I did before I transitioned to a plant-based diet.

I added 1 kg of muscle in under 21 days and got into great shape using my 90 Day Plant Powered Shred online programme, using the same techniques I once did when I ate meat.

0 Days   7 Days   14 Days   21 Days (18 Days technically)   End of Cycle 2   End of Cycle 3

I've also had many amazing results with clients coaching them on a plant-based diet and, aside from the improvements to the way they look externally, there is a renewed vibrancy of spirit they feel and a glow that shines from them, once they embrace a plant-based diet.

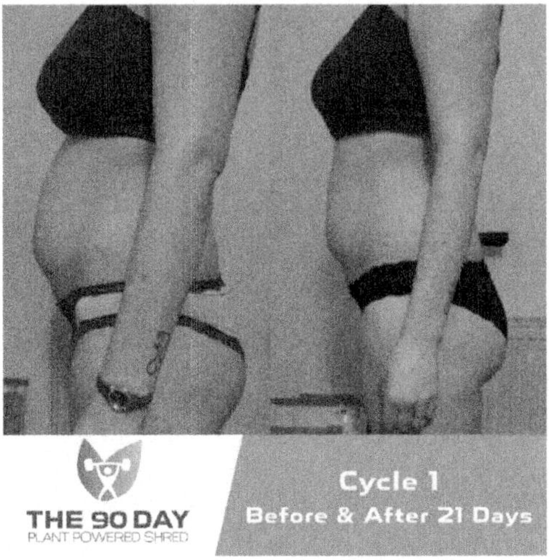

At the time of writing this I feel as fit as I did over ten years ago. I turned 40 in 2018, and although my goals have changed, I train and play sport four to five times a week and enjoy the energy and recovery that my plant-powered diet brings.

I feel the fittest and healthiest I ever have, but the effects on my health and well-being have not only been felt physically. I now feel 'spiritually lighter' knowing that I am no longer contributing to one of the most damaging human activities on the planet; I think my subconscious always knew, even if I wasn't aware of it at the time.

CHAPTER RECIPE

SUPER-CHARGED GREEN SMOOTHIE

Generally, if I'm having a pre-workout smoothie then I like to have a medium-to-low carbohydrate content (apple/pear), a higher fat content (half avocado), plenty of amino acids and protein (spirulina and protein powder) and of course something to give me a kick (matcha and/or cordyceps).

Servings: 1

Ingredients:

- ½ avocado
- 1 big handful organic kale or spinach
- 1 scoop plant protein powder
- 1 tsp spirulina
- 1 tsp matcha and/or cordyceps mushrooms
- 1 apple or pear (destalked)
- 300 ml filtered water

You will need:

- 1 high-powered blender

Cooking Method:

1. Add the water first to the blender, then the rest of the ingredients. Blend on full power and enjoy 30–40 minutes before training.

CHAPTER 20

SHOULD I SUPPLEMENT?

There are so many supplements out there to spend your hard-earned cash on – trust me, I've spent thousands of pounds over the years and to be honest, most are either unnecessary or have very little impact.

When it comes to supplements these days, I always ask myself, 'Is the juice worth the squeeze?' Am I going to see a return on my investment with regards health impact, physical gains and enjoyment of consumption? Some super foods I actually really enjoy having in the cupboards as they make cooking creative.

I have already given you my list of favourite super foods, so this chapter will focus on those much-needed micronutrients and workout supplementation.

Micronutrients

To avoid potential deficiencies on a plant-based diet there are a few supplements that it is worth you getting hold off just to avoid deficiencies. But it is always worth getting your blood tested to see if and what you are deficient in first, as we all utilise nutrients differently from one another, and this could save you lots of time and money by giving your body exactly what it needs.

B12 – Men and Women – Supplement or Fortified Foods

B12 is primarily responsible for healthy red blood cell

formation and plays an important role in the health of nerve tissue and brain function. Usually when people are deficient in B12 they are fatigued and experience a very weakened immune system, meaning they are susceptible to colds, flus and other symptoms.

Bacteria are responsible for producing vitamin B12. Animals get their vitamin B12 from eating foods that are contaminated with vitamin B12 from the soil etc. and then the animal becomes a source of vitamin B12. Plant foods do not contain vitamin B12 except when they are contaminated by microorganisms.

On a vegan diet the best ways to obtain an adequate supply of vitamin B12 is to eat foods fortified with it or to supplement directly with it.

Nutritional yeast flakes and yeast extract are good vegan sources of B12 to have in your diet and can be added to meals and recipes very easily. I add yeast flakes to many of my meals as a topping and you can also make a great vegan parmesan for pasta using cashews and yeast flakes.

Just look for plant milks, yoghurts, breakfast cereals, spreads, yeast extracts and nutritional yeast products that are fortified with vitamin B12 or buy a good quality vegan B12 supplement.

Vitamins and trace minerals are routinely added in almost every commercial feed for all animal species, making their manufacturing, distribution, marketing and sales a global industry worth billions.

Many farmed animals receive B12 supplementation. For ruminant animals (four stomach compartments) like cows and sheep, they can produce B12 through bacteria in the rumen, but they need cobalt in their diet to do so. Since lots of soil is depleted of cobalt, cows and sheep need a cobalt supplement. Most cattle are not grass-fed, but grain-fed, so their cobalt-supplemented feed may not provide them a significant amount of B12, in which case they need a B12 supplement.

Pigs and chickens are not ruminants, so they get B12 from their diet. Since their feed consists of grains, soy and other plant foods (which are not a source of B12), they need supplementation.

The most common trace minerals added to diets are iron, zinc, copper, manganese, iodine and selenium, while other water-soluble vitamins, such as riboflavin, pantothenic acid, niacin, vitamin B12 and all of the fat-soluble vitamins (A, D, E, and K) are routinely added to diets for monogastric animals.

Many argue that a vegan diet is inadequate because it needs supplementation. Well then, the same could be said of an omnivorous diet that contains farmed animal products.

DHA – Men and Women – Supplement or Wholefoods.
EPA and DHA are essential fatty acids (omega 3s), mostly widely obtained from oily fish and fish oil supplements on a non-vegan diet.

Now while we can get a good fatty acid profile from many superfoods such as hemp, flax and chia seeds, it is harder to increase levels of the essential fatty acid DHA due to the inefficient conversion process that needs to happen when converting the plant-based ALA form to EPA and DHA which is needed by the body.

But we can avoid a deficiency here by supplementing with good quality micro algae oil, which of course removes the middleman (fish) and avoids ingesting many of the toxins found in our oceans.

Vitamin D3 – Men and Women – Sunlight, Fortified Foods or Supplements

Primarily obtained from sunlight and then unfortunately secondary from animal products, this is an essential vitamin to ensure you have during the winter months, especially if you live in a country far from the equator.

Make sure you get a vegan D3 supplement as normal D3 supplements are obtained through a process involving sheep lanolin, a waxy substance found in sheep's skin.

Vegan D3 sources come from 'lichen' a unique type of plant that has a symbiotic relationship between fungus and algae.

Iron – Women Mainly – Supplements, Fortified Foods or Wholefoods

The major function of iron is to combine with protein and copper in making haemoglobin. Iron provides numerous beneficial roles in maintaining well-being, including enhancing the immune system, energy production, growth in children and resistance to stress and disease.

Iron is another tricky one to look out for in your plant-powered diet. Although it is super high in many green leafy vegetables, it is a kind of iron called 'non-heme iron', which is not absorbed as well by the body as the iron derived from animal sources called 'heme iron'. But this could be a good thing.

Heme iron maybe absorbed better, but studies have shown that heme iron consumption can increase the risk of serious diseases. One study found heme iron increased the risk of coronary heart disease by 57%. Other studies have also shown a correlation between heme iron and increased risk of colon cancer. This is particularly true for red meat.

Good plant sources of iron include dried fruits, whole grains (including wholemeal bread), nuts, green leafy vegetables, potatoes, seeds and pulses. Other foods rich in iron, but which are usually eaten in smaller amounts, include soya, some flours, parsley, watercress, dark chocolate, black molasses and edible seaweeds.

To increase the absorption of iron, combine it with foods or supplements that are high in vitamin C, such as broccoli and citrus fruits or superfoods such as goji berries, baobab and camu camu.

Iron toxicity is more of a concern in men than women. So, men should test for deficiency before supplementing with iron.

Zinc – Men Mainly – Supplement or Wholefoods

Zinc is needed for healthy cell division and it acts like an antioxidant, fighting free radical damage and slowing the ageing process, improving immune function, wound healing and reproductive health. Zinc benefits hormonal health and fertility because it plays an important role in hormone production, including increasing testosterone naturally and can be harder to obtain on a vegan diet.

Zinc also plays a part in modulating the brain and body's response to stress and a deficiency could lead to symptoms of anxiety and depression.

Foods that are high in zinc such as beans and legumes also contain phytates or phytic acid which can prevent or slow down absorption.

Caffeine can also prevent the absorption of minerals such as zinc, so it is advisable not to drink a caffeinated drink within two hours of eating as it may affect the absorption of zinc from your meal.

Pumpkin seeds, hemp seeds, chickpeas, cashews and nutritional yeast flakes are good sources of zinc.

Men's RDA is 11mg whereas women's is 8 mg, although women should go up to 11 mg if pregnant and 12mg if lactating.

But it is also important to check stress levels and gut health as this will lead to depletion and malabsorption issues.

Iodine – Men and Women – Supplements, Fortified Foods or Wholefoods

Iodine is a mineral found in some foods.The body needs iodine to make thyroid hormones. These hormones control the body's metabolism and many other important functions. The body also needs thyroid hormones for proper bone and brain development during pregnancy and infancy.

Your thyroid gland uses it to make thyroid hormones, which help control growth, repair damaged cells and support a healthy metabolism.

Low iodine and hypothyroidism can show symptoms such as fatigue, depression and forgetfulness, hair weakness and hair loss, dry skin, weight gain, cold intolerance and constipation.

Sea vegetables are a great source of iodine such as seaweed, kombu kelp, wakame and nori. Iodised salt is also a very good source of iodine, as are prunes on a plant-based diet.

Try and buy supplements that are derived from wholefood sources and do not contain any additional non-active ingredients such as fillers and bulking agents. Supplements derived from wholefood plant sources generally have better absorption (bioavailability) which means you need less. Have a look around, there are some great brands out there.

Training Supplementation

There are probably three basic supplements that I take to support intensive training cycles:

Protein Powder

Gone are the days when I used to just drink a protein powder on its own, because on its own it is nutritionally inferior. It contains no fibre, so will go through you quickly without satisfying your hunger and because they can be watery and unfulfilling to drink. These days I always use it as part of a nutrient-dense smoothie, along with combinations of fruits, vegetables, nuts and seeds, so that I not only get my protein intake but all my other essential macro and micronutrients (vitamins and minerals) to help support my health, growth and recovery.

Creatine

This has been a game changer for me since going vegan, as we are unable to obtain creatine from plant sources, so it must be synthesised to make it vegan-certified. Creatine is formed in the human body and thus also in animal protein. It is used for energy production, specifically for muscular strength, speed and power. I usually add 10 g of this either before, during or after in a workout drink or my post-workout smoothie.

Cell volume is critical for getting amino acids inside the cell. It's also the fundamental property of substances like creatine. Creatine is what's known as a 'cell volumiser' which means it directly increases cell volume by pulling additional water into the cell when it's absorbed.

Due to lacking a large intestine and needing to use the toilet approximately eight times per day, I can lose a lot of water. And as our muscle cells are made up of mainly water, I can lose muscle fullness and weight very quickly, along with amino acid uptake for growth and recovery, if I don't manage my hydration levels.

Supplementing with creatine really helps my body to maintain my water balance, muscle fullness, strength in the gym and my potential for muscle growth.

Top Tip: Try adding spirulina into your pre-workout smoothie like the Super-Charged Green Smoothie in the previous chapter, as it contains the amino acids glycine, arginine and methionine, which are used by the body to naturally create creatine.

BCAAs (Branched Chain Amino Acids)

This refers to three amino acids: leucine, isoleucine, and valine. For people with low dietary protein intake, BCAA supplementation can promote muscle protein synthesis and increase muscle growth over time.

I sometimes use a powdered drink of BCAAs along with my creatine to have during training. This supports energy production and prevents muscle breakdown while training.

If I am looking for a more wholefood source of BCAAs, or if I run out of my supplements, then again I use spirulina, as it contains all the BCAAs, including the amino acids needed for creatine production. Add to water with a drop of natural sweetener such as agave or maple syrup to drink during training.

As with everything I've spoken about in this book, keep it Simple and Sustainable, also question whether you need all those expensive workout supplements. They are not necessary to live a healthy life, but the basic supplements mentioned above can help to support those people with active lifestyles.

Remember what the word supplement means…

'A thing added to something else in order to complete or enhance it.'

Supplements might give you a slight edge, but only if you already have the solid foundation of a structured training programme and a good wholefood plant-based diet. They are NOT a magic bullet, and won't work on their own.

Get the basics right first!

CHAPTER RECIPE

FLASHY BEANS ON TOAST

Who doesn't love beans on toast? Well it just gets better when you make a fresh version and add in extra plants to really make it a delicious and nutritious start to the day.

For those with smaller appetites, halve the amount of beans. Also try making this with cannellini or pinto beans as well.

Servings: 1

Ingredients:
- 4–5 mushrooms sliced
- 230 g of drained and cooked butter beans (approx. 1 tin or packet drained)
- 1 tbsp coconut or avocado oil
- 1 tsp smoked paprika
- 1 tbsp apple cider vinegar
- 1 tsp dark miso
- 1 small handful of spinach
- ½ tin organic chopped tomatoes
- ½ onion
- 2 slices of toasted sourdough or rye bread
- 2 tsp basil pesto
- Salt and pepper to season

You will need:
- 1 frying pan preferably with lid
- 1 wooden stirring spoon
- 1 sharp knife

- 1 chopping board

Cooking Method:

1. Pan fry the onions with the oil and a little water on a medium heat with the lid on until they are soft and slightly browned.
2. Add the chopped mushrooms and cook until the water has evaporated from them.
3. Add the ½ tin chopped tomatoes, paprika, apple cider vinegar, the dark miso and heat through.
4. Add the spinach and the butter beans. Cook until the spinach has wilted and the beans have warmed through. Season with black pepper and salt to taste and a squeeze of lemon juice.
5. Toast the sourdough or rye bread and spread each slice with 1 tsp of dairy-free basil pesto.
6. Serve the bean mixture on top, salivate and enjoy!

SUMMARY

After reading Part 2 I hope that you now have a good understanding of the basic mechanisms that need to be harnessed to improve your body, and that I have proved the following points:

Vegans do NOT need to work out or train differently

Just because vegans do not eat meat, fish or dairy, it doesn't mean that they are handicapped. It just means that we have chosen to improve our own health and physical well-being while minimising the suffering that is being caused to animals and the environment.

A plant-based diet, contrary to misguided belief (which is changing), does not impair performance and ability but can improve and enhance both performance and recovery.

The same rules still apply to burning body fat and building muscle; it's just the source of nutrients that has changed.

You can get all the PROTEIN you need from a plant-powered diet

Humans, no matter what diet they eat, need an abundance of certain nutrients to survive optimally. Most of those vital nutrients must come from plant-based food sources.

Plants contain all the protein and essential amino acids we need in our diet. We need less than we've been led to believe thanks to our obsession to build muscle and the marketing strategy that more protein equals better.

You can improve your PERFORMANCE on a plant-powered diet

The same underlying issues that affect athletic performance such as blood flow, inflammation, hormone levels, etc. also affect our basic health, including sexual function, body composition and cognitive function.

A plant-powered diet can improve all areas of your life, your health, body composition and performance.

All essential amino acids originate from plants. Either you eat the plant, or you eat the animal that ate the plant. Either way, the essential amino acids came from the plant.

PART 3

PROTEIN AND OUR PLANET

"He who has health, has hope;
he who has hope, has everything." Thomas
Carlyle

The main reason for going vegan myself and for writing this book is that I want to try and live a life that reduces the trauma and suffering on the world around me, and I want to show you that there is an alternative option. It's not a perfect solution – nothing is – but it's about making positive steps towards a better future, Progress not Perfection.

We are fixated on our own individual health, which is understandable as it's the only thing we have direct control over in our lives, but if we are all truly connected then surely our own individual health and our collective health as human beings is also connected and that each one is a reflection of the other.

Can we really experience optimal individual health if the health of others and the planet around us is crumbling? And vice versa, can the planet ever achieve full optimal health if as individuals we are not caring enough for our own health and well-being?

This, I feel, is where the conversation needs to extend now, away from just 'is this diet/way of living good or bad for me?' but instead 'is this way of living good or bad for myself, others and the environment?' When it comes down to it, even if you're experiencing the best health you possibly can and look amazing, what good is that if everything around you is crumbling?

At the time of writing this, approximately 3% of the global population identifies themselves as being vegan. This is a drop in the ocean, but the good news is that it is growing rapidly.

If approximately 97% of the global population still consume animal products, then a huge part of the damage caused to our environment is through the demand for meat and other animal-derived products.

Just because we've been doing something for thousands of years, it doesn't make it right. As we evolve in consciousness, so does our empathy and compassion for others. Slavery, apartheid, gay rights, women's rights, etc. are all great examples of how we've evolved with our morality and look back with horror at our past actions and beliefs. I feel we will do the same with animal agriculture and the abuse we have inflicted on animals.

This is what we will explore in Part 3. I will join the dots and highlight the impact that our obsession with individual health is having on our health collectively and globally.

CHAPTER 21

THE FITNESS INDUSTRY

"Education is the most powerful weapon,
which you can use to change the world."
Nelson Mandela

Unless you've been living under a rock for the last 10–20 years then you'll have noticed the ever-increasing interest from the public for health and fitness, gyms, classes, bodybuilding, cross fit, etc. It was just a matter of time before it spilled out from the US and really took hold of the rest of the world, especially the UK, where I have grown up with my own passion for the fitness world. As my own awareness of it has developed, I've witnessed it growing all around me, and the stats don't lie.

The global health and fitness industry is worth over $83 billion and there are over 162 million gym members worldwide. In the UK, one in seven people have a gym membership.

NOTE: Remember approximately 97% of these gym members will consume animal protein in some shape or form to aid their performance, growth and recovery.

Social Media

Social media has had a huge effect on this, especially on

platforms such as YouTube and Instagram, where users regularly post-workout videos and pictures of their beautiful bodies, achieved through hard, dedicated work in the gym. Just by doing a quick search on a few hashtags on Instagram you can clearly see the popularity of certain topics and the post figures relating to them.

At the time of the last update of this manuscript we can see the popularity of certain hashtags on Instagram.

December 2020
#Fitness – 426mn
#Bodybuilding – 111mn
#Vegan – 104mn
#CrossFit – 59mn
#VeganFitness – 1.9mn
#VeganBodybuilding – 965k

We can see just how popular fitness and bodybuilding is, especially when we compare them to VeganFitness and VeganBodybuilding. The #Bodybuilding is also out-performing #Vegan, which is amazing when you consider that bodybuilding is a fringe sport and veganism is a global movement.

So to give you perspective, remember that 97% of those who posted under the #Fitness and #Bodybuilding hashtags will consume animal protein in some shape or form to aid their performance, growth and recovery.

Bodybuilding Federations in the UK

Bodybuilding has been around for a long time but used to be

very much out of the mainstream. Now it is getting a huge amount of attention and publicity thanks to the global surge in popularity through social media and the introduction of certain competitions and classes along with the more 'traditional' bodybuilding classes and competitions.

For instance, the WBFF, which originated in the US, is now a huge global federation with fitness and bodybuilding shows in the US, Canada, UK, Holland, Brazil, Hong Kong, India, Australia, South Korea, China, Singapore, South Africa and Turkey.

Part of the reason for their success is that they appeal to a much wider demographic than the traditional bodybuilding shows. This is due to the rise and popularity of their Male and Female Fitness Model categories, which champion a 'cover model' physique that is much more attainable for most people and therefore gets much more attention from a broader audience.

Here's an approximate list of a few of the fitness and bodybuilding federations and shows in just the UK, and an approximate number of categories per show:

UKBFF – approx. 21 shows and 26 categories
NABBA – approx. 20 shows and 12 categories
BNBF – approx. 9 shows and 11 categories
NPA – approx. 7 shows
Miami Pro – 2 shows and 6 Categories
WBFF (Global) – approx. 29 shows, 2 in UK and 6 categories
IFBB (Pro Shows Globally) – approx. 46 shows

You can see that within each federation there are multiple shows that go on throughout the year or season and within each show there are multiple categories, that also contain many competitors. I am attempting to show you that 97% of all those competitors will also favour animal protein sources over plant protein, and in fact I would say that figure is closer to 98–99% due to the popularity of animal-based protein sources in the bodybuilding world.

CrossFit

Another huge trend in the fitness industry and thriving fitness subculture is CrossFit. We have seen a huge rise in the popularity of CrossFit since it was founded in 2000. CrossFit is a constantly changing mix of aerobic exercise, gymnastics, and weightlifting, with the focus on physical performance rather than physical appearance, although the top CrossFit athletes, male and female, have incredibly strong, muscular and athletic physiques as a by-product of their focus on performance.

The CrossFit Open, which takes place every February, is a five-week fitness competition which tests strength, endurance and aspects of gymnastics, with over half a million athletes worldwide taking part in the workouts that are posted on the CrossFit website. Competitors from around the globe then submit their times and results, and everyone ends up on the worldwide leader board.

The leaders after the initial CrossFit Open all go onto the Regionals, held across the world, and the winners of those events end up at the CrossFit Games in the US during the summer, with the aim to crown a male and female 'the fittest in the world'.

CrossFit has over 13,000 gyms in more than 120 countries, and there are an estimated 4 million CrossFit devotees.

Another common nutrition theme in CrossFit as with bodybuilding is the recommendation of animal-based protein sources, with the Paleo diet being a very popular practice amongst the CrossFit world. The Paleo diet focuses on animal protein, fats and vegetables with very limited to no starchy carbohydrates and no dairy, believing this to be the way our ancestors ate.

Remember approximately 97% of those who follow CrossFit will probably consume animal protein in some shape or form with only a small percentage following a plant-based diet, if we are to go by statistics.

Are you starting to see where I'm going with this?

Another hugely popular and ever-growing global industry of fitness that relies heavily on protein derived from animals.

CHAPTER RECIPE

BLACK BEAN PROTEIN BROWNIE

These brownies are amazing, and you wouldn't even guess that they contain any black beans, which add extra fibre and protein to the mix. Along with an added scoop of plant protein powder (vanilla, chocolate, salted caramel, toffee fudge etc or similar flavours), you've got yourself a super delicious and nutritious post-workout treat.

Servings: 12–16

Ingredients:

- 450 g cooked and drained black beans
- 120 g coconut sugar
- 30 g almond, cashew, pecan or peanut butter
- 6 tbsp raw cacao powder
- 2 tbsp ground flax seeds
- 2 tbsp vanilla extract
- 1 scoop plant protein powder (vanilla, chocolate, salted caramel, toffee fudge, etc.)
- ¼ tsp salt
- ½ tsp baking soda
- 90 g coarsely chopped dark chocolate (70–90%)

You will need:

- 9-inch square baking dish
- Baking paper
- Food processor
- Chopping board and knife

Cooking Method:

1. Preheat the oven to 180°C and line a 9-inch square baking dish with parchment paper. In a large food processor, process the black beans until smooth.
2. To the pureed black beans, add in the almond butter, cacao powder, ground flax, vanilla, sugar, protein powder, salt and baking soda. Process until a very smooth and thick batter is formed, stopping to scrape down the sides at least once to make sure everything is mixed evenly.
3. Add the chopped dark chocolate to the batter and pulse a few times to mix in. Use a spatula to scoop the batter into the lined 9-inch baking dish. The batter will be rather thick, so you'll need to use the spatula to spread it evenly into the pan.
4. Bake until the top begins to crack and the centre feels relatively firm to a light touch, about 30 minutes. Allow the brownies to cool completely before attempting to cut them into squares, as they are very fragile when warm.
5. Serve at room temperature and store any leftovers in an airtight container in the fridge for up to a week.

CHAPTER 22

THE PROTEIN OBSESSION

My body is a temple, not a tomb.

From the previous chapter we can see that the fitness industry is a rapidly expanding culture, on and offline. Within that there are also the rapidly expanding subcultures of fitness modelling, bodybuilding and CrossFit that all promote a diet high in animal protein to their devotees as the best way to support their physiques, performance and muscular gains, at an amateur and professional level.

As our obsession for improved physical prowess and performance has increased, so has our obsession for the consumption of protein and as we have been traditionally programmed to believe this must be obtained from animal sources, you can see how the rise of this obsession has led to an increase in the demand for meat.

Body Image + Performance + Fitness = Protein Obsession

Where did it begin?

In the 1990s we had a huge surge in the 'anti-fat' movement and the belief that all of the growing health problems in society was the cause of fats.

Then as we hit the turn of the century 'Carbphobia' crept in and we shifted away from the belief that fat was our evil arch enemy to believing now that it was in fact carbohydrates that were causing all of our health issues. And so the low-carb craze began as people started to avoid carbohydrates, believing that they were the source of health problems and weight gain.

Then seemingly out of nowhere, protein rose up to become the cure-all macronutrient, that it would increase muscle mass, give you the body you'd always wanted, banish unwanted body fat forever and improve your health. You just needed to eat more of it!

Arise King Protein

Along with this popularity came the increase in availability of protein powders, specifically whey protein powders, a waste by-product of the scary dairy industry, and an efficient way of adding additional protein into your diet through shakes and smoothies.

Then it became common place for almost all pre-packaged foods to be marketed as having 'added protein' in them, as the popularity and demand for more protein grew.

We have now ended up with added protein in:

- Smoothies
- Snack bars
- Cookies
- Peanut butter
- Pancakes
- Puddings

You name it, we've added protein to it, with the common misguided belief that 'more equals better', which seems to be a very human trait. Protein has become a great marketing buzz word, just like the term's gluten-free, dairy-free, organic, cold pressed, raw, and even vegan.

CBD is the latest buzz word and supplement to put on the ingredients list of products. Don't get me wrong, I'm a big believer in CBD oil to help with many ailments but companies are now adding it into everything from bath salts to tampons, I kid you not!

All these terms are now used liberally on products, not necessarily to benefit your health, but to benefit the sales and bottom lines of companies. As the demand and trends for these terms grow, so do their sales.

Do We Need all that Additional Protein?

So, with all that additional protein that we 'need' in various food products would you think that we are in danger of becoming protein deficient?

74,171,872,986 land animals
slaughtered in 2016

Yet we slaughter over 74 billion land animals globally every year for their meat consumption (over 150 billion including marine life), which would suggest to me that we are doing just fine with our protein consumption and really don't need more of it. Just to put that figure in perspective, that's the same amount as if you were to wipe out the total population of humans over nine times every year.

Wouldn't it be great if we didn't need to add additional protein to food products or slaughter billions of animals for our protein consumption?

I wonder where we could find a natural source of amino acids, fibre, fats, carbohydrates, vitamins and minerals, that is balanced and ready for us to eat for optimal health?

We already do, in nature and from plants.

VEGAN MYTH BUSTING
BUT EATING MEAT IS A SIGN OF MASCULINITY!

This common misconception and argument used to back up male eating behaviours must come from an age when we were hunter gatherers, going out onto the plains to courageously hunt beasts to feed our families and tribes, giving us purpose and meaning, challenging our natural hunting skills, giving us a definitive role for male bravery in society.

In modern society, the nearest we get to hunter gathering is by stealthily tracking a slow-moving joint of beef wrapped in cellophane on aisle 28 of a supermarket. We pounce and bravely tackle the already-dead and packaged piece of flesh, that no longer resembles an animal, dragging it to the checkout over our shoulders, where we scan the barcode and swipe our debit cards, walking out of the supermarket to our parked car, proud of the fact we have just provided essential nourishment for our family, who now won't go hungry for a few hours.

Masculinity – 'possession of the qualities traditionally associated with men.'

Strong, stable, reliable, courage, protector, loyalty, compassionate, caring are all qualities that I associate with being a man. I don't need to consume meat in any shape or form to reinforce those qualities, there's nothing strong, courageous or compassionate about 'supermarket hunter gathering'.

"In our entire recorded history, 619,000,000 humans have been killed by war, we kill the same number of animals every 3 days."
Dominion *(2018 documentary)*

THE HUMANE HOAX

One of the arguments for continuing meat consumption is to only eat meat from 'humane sources'. I know, because this was my intention when I started my journey. I didn't intend to go fully plant based and thought that if I bought free-range or grass-fed animals that my conscience would be clearer.

Firstly, whether you eat factory-farmed, grass-fed or free-range meat, the animals all still end up in the same slaughterhouses, bound for the same traumatic fate; and just because we've 'allowed' the animals to live a comfortable life does that give us the right to end it prematurely? it seems pretty underhand to treat an animal as a friend for a short while, loving it as a pet, while planning to only let it fulfil not even 10% of its potential lifespan, just so you can have a good-quality end product and a clearer conscience.

Just because you can humanely kill something, it doesn't mean you should.

If someone broke into your house and shot you in your sleep, murdering you without you knowing it, would that make the act of murdering someone any more acceptable?

LIFE EXPECTANCY OF FARMED ANIMALS

The reality of farming animals for consumption is that to produce a good quality end product your meat must be tender and tasty, which directly correlates to the age of the animal when it is slaughtered. So even though it may have been allowed to run around in the fields 'free', fed grass and cared for by the farmer, maybe even massaged in the case of Japanese wagyu beef (who also are given an extra year to live – how lucky they are), the animals farmed and killed for their meat are slaughtered long before they reach their potential lifespan.

Here are some examples:

Caged Chickens – Live up to 18 months, of a potential 10-year lifespan.

Beef Cattle – Live up to 18–24 months, of a potential 15–20-year lifespan.

Japanese Wagyu Beef – Live up to 36 months, of a potential 15–20-year lifespan.

Dairy Cows – Live up to 5–6 years old, of a potential 15–20-year lifespan.

Calves (reared for veal) – Live up to 18 months, of a potential 20-year lifespan.

Piglets (whole suckling pig) – Live up to 2 weeks, of a potential 20-year lifespan.

Pigs – Live up to 4–6 months, of a potential 20-year lifespan.

Pigs (female) – Live up to 18 months, of a potential 20-year lifespan.

They endure 3–5 pregnancies before being slaughtered

Lambs – 3–5 months, of a potential 10-year lifespan. Sometimes they are slaughtered as young as 6 weeks old.

Fish – Although it's harder for us to relate to fish as a species feeling pain etc., they are still plucked from their environment in vast numbers, crushed in nets under the weight of other fish and generally die through suffocation.

Looking at that list above, we can see that in general animals bred for their meat don't make it past 10% of their potential lifespan. At least animals living in the wild have a chance to live a life naturally, without the dates of their birth and death planned into a calendar.

The average life expectancy of a human these days is 79 years old. If I was not allowed to live past 10% of my potential lifespan then I would have been slaughtered when I was about seven or eight years old, 32 years ago and I wouldn't be sat here writing this book, nor would I have been able to experience life and this wonderful planet.

There's no humane way to kill something, that wants to live.

VEGAN MYTH BUSTING
ANIMALS DON'T EXPERIENCE EMOTIONAL ATTACHMENT

They experience it on a deeper level than you think. The need for attachment is genetically imprinted in all mammals for survival purposes.

It's a mechanism that helps humans and animals to survive. Without that innate need to attach ourselves to another being for food, love and support we would not survive those early years and neither would animals, especially in the wild.

This means that detaching an infant from its mother in any

species is traumatic and it interferes with natural survival instincts that occur immediately after birth.

So now look at the scenario that surrounds dairy farming:

A female cow must be pregnant to produce milk. She must first be artificially inseminated against her will to make her pregnant, then when she goes through that whole pregnancy and gives birth, her child is taken away from her every time.

The mother and child will suffer the trauma of not just this experience but the trauma that their lives then lead to.

For the mother, continued forced insemination against her will (rape?), pregnancy and child kidnapping to produce milk until there's nothing left in her and she is sold for meat.

For the baby, if a girl she'll go into the same existence as her mother; if a boy, then he'll either be killed or forced into the veal industry, where he will live a short life confined to a cramped living space and then slaughtered for his flesh just 6–12 months after his birth.

That innocent glass of milk we grew up on has a very sinister back story that no one tells you about or connects you with.

Is it Worth it?

My question for you to ponder until the end of this book is this.

So, if we know that we can build the healthy, athletic, muscular and high-performing body we need on a plant-based diet then is it worth all this trauma, suffering, loss of life and potential damage to our own health, environment and food chain?

Remember the first Plant Powered Principle...

'Reduce Trauma and Suffering'

CHAPTER RECIPE

CANNELLINI BEANS, COURGETTI WITH TOMATO AND FENNEL PESTO

This dish is so simple, fresh and tasty, bursting with Italian colours and flavours. I did cheat slightly by using a shop-bought pesto when I first made this but it was so good that I had to make my own homemade tomato and fennel pesto recipe for the dish.

Servings: 2

Ingredients:

- 1 x onion finely sliced
- 1 x clove of garlic lovingly sliced
- 1 x sweet red pepper sliced or cubed
- ½ aubergine cubed
- 1 x tin of chopped organic tomatoes
- 1 x pack cooked organic cannellini beans (washed)
- 1 x spiralised courgette
- 2 tbsp tomato and fennel pesto
- Salt and pepper to taste
- Topped with cashew parmesan

Fresh Tomato and Fennel Pesto

- 100 g fresh cherry or pomodoro tomatoes (small and sweet essentially)
- 50 g sundried tomatoes
- 1 small fresh chilli
- 1 small handful of fennel leaves (organic or wild preferably)

- 4 tbsp extra virgin olive oil
- 30 g organic almonds
- Salt to taste

You will need:

- 1 spiraliser to make the courgetti
- 1 large frying pan with lid
- 1 blender for the pesto
- 1 wooden spoon

Cooking Method:

1. To make the pesto, just add all the ingredients to a food processor or blender, and blend until smooth
2. Sauté the onion and garlic in a little oil and splash of water, put the lid on and leave for a minute.
3. Then add the red pepper, aubergine, a splash more water to help cook and place the lid back on for a couple of minutes.
4. Add the pesto and leave to cook for a minute.
5. Add the tin of tomatoes and simmer for 5 minutes.
6. During the above, simmer spiralise one courgette and put to one side.
7. Add the beans to the pan, salt, pepper and taste, warm the beans through and then add the courgetti until softened.
8. Serve and top with cashew parmesan (made by blending a handful of cashews, yeast flakes and a pinch of salt).

CHAPTER 23

THE ENVIRONMENT

"Look deep into Nature, and then you will understand everything better."
Albert Einstein

The argument to me is very simple and logical. It's just basic mathematics that will tell you that we cannot maintain our current trajectory, with the habits we have; all it needs is a little foresight of cause and effect to see where we are heading. Consider this:

1. We live on a finite planet, it is limited in size and space.
2. Human births per day are approximately 185,000.
3. Human deaths per day are approximately 75,000.
4. Meaning we are adding approximately 110,000 new humans per day to a planet that is limited in size and space.
5. We can also see that the demand for meat is increasing, to feed these extra mouths that are being bought up in the 'meat is best' belief system.
6. So, we are losing space on this planet to not only an increased number of humans but an increased number of farmed animals, not to mention the additional crops grown to feed those animals and the resources needed to support their lives, such as land and fresh water.

7. This means that most of those animals will be kept in smaller and smaller areas to accommodate them, leading to more horrific living conditions.
8. These cramped and traumatic living conditions will lead to a greater risk of disease spreading.
9. The greater risk of disease will lead to an increased number of antibiotics needed for prevention and an increased need for supplements and hormones to ensure growth and profit is sustained.
10. This greater use of antibiotics could lead to an increased risk of resistant diseases that could be deadly to humans who consume meat from this part of the food chain.
11. We are either wiped out by a disease that our antibiotics cannot treat, or we eventually run out of space.

Whether you like it or not, a reduction in the meat we consume is going to happen, it must happen. Better that we all get on board sooner than later.

The actual planet is going to be fine, it was here long before us and will be here long after we are gone but the atmosphere that supports life is not quite as sturdy. It's this atmosphere and the synergistic relationship between all life on our planet that is so crucial for our survival and it's this relationship that is most at risk of becoming unbalanced.

All animals and wildlife work together in harmony, only taking the resources that are needed, nothing more, nothing less. Even without conscious thought (or so we think), all other animals are genetically hardwired to know their role in the cycle of life, unlike us where we seem to believe that we can 'cheat' the system, outwit nature and take more than we need.

Due to the ever-increasing global population and the increased demand for resources, we are using more than we can give back. Our debt to nature is rising and we are already having trouble paying back what we owe. This seems to be a common problem with our species, you just need to take one look at the ongoing global financial problems to see that this habit of taking more than we need has reached epidemic proportions and flows into all areas of our existence.

The Growing Demand for Meat

At the time of writing this the global population is approximately 7.8 billion and growing by at least 200,000 each day. That's over 73 million new humans on our planet every year. Also remember that approximately 95–97% of the global population consume animal products.

Many scientists think Earth has a maximum carrying capacity of 9 billion to 10 billion people and as the Harvard University sociobiologist Edward O. Wilson pointed out in his book *The Future of Life* (Knopf, 2002), "The constraints of the biosphere are fixed."

We have a finite supply of freshwater and the Earth's resources can only be stretched so far in terms of food production.

"If everyone agreed to become vegetarian, leaving little or nothing for livestock, the present 1.4 billion hectares of arable land (3.5 billion acres) would support about 10 billion people," Wilson wrote.

Aside from the huge problem of producing enough food to support life, there's an economic problem. There are approximately 1.3 billion people employed in the livestock sector worldwide, with the global meat, poultry and seafood market expected to reach 7.3 trillion US dollars by 2025. The industries' revenue is anticipated to grow to such levels due to the increasing population and demand for meat, poultry and seafood products.

With such a huge industry at the forefront of our environmental problems, it will take time to slow it down, unravel and change its habits.

In 2016, the world's meat production was estimated at 317.17 million metric tons, with industrial countries the biggest meat eaters.

Industrialised Countries: 76.2 kg
Developing Countries: 33.5 kg

**avg per person/year*

A big factor in our global consumption of meat is a socio-economic issue, with the wealthiest nations consuming over twice the amount of meat that poorer countries consume. It's more expensive for these countries to farm and consume so they rely heavily on plant-based protein sources, which are cheaper and easier to produce, though for many poor farmers in developing countries livestock are also a source of renewable energy and a source of organic fertiliser for their crops.

In North America or Europe, a cow consumes about 75 kg to 300 kg of dry feed — grass or grain – to produce 1 kg of protein. In sub-Saharan Africa, a cow might need 500 kg to 2,000 kg of dry feed to produce 1 kg of protein, because of the poor feed quality in arid countries and because of the high mortality rates in herds of often undernourished and sick animals.

Land and Pollution

Livestock now uses 30% of the Earth's entire ice-free land surface, with another 33% of arable land used for feed crop production, turning our beautiful and naturally diverse planet into a gigantic farm. These herds of livestock also cause widespread degradation of land through overgrazing, compaction and erosion.

The livestock business is also the most damaging sector to the Earth's increasingly scarce water resources, contributing to water pollution, eutrophication (excessive richness of nutrients due to run-off which cause a dense growth of plant life) and the degeneration of coral reefs.

Animal agriculture is responsible for 20%–33% of all freshwater consumption in the world today and one-third of the global water footprint of animal production is related to beef cattle.

The major pollutants to water sources come from animal wastes, antibiotics and hormones, chemicals from tanneries, fertilisers and the pesticides used to spray feed crops.

Animals in the meat and dairy industry also now account for 20% of all terrestrial animal biomass on our planet, needing vast swathes of land for feed crops that contribute to biodiversity loss as more land is needed to produce monocrops to support and graze them.

Most of the rainforest deforestation is driven by human activity. The leading drivers being agriculture and cattle ranching for both international and local markets. Although much of the food production is not consumed locally but is instead exported overseas. That means although you may live thousands of miles away from the rainforests and feel that you have no connection to what is happening, you are partly responsible for these incredibly beautiful and most importantly, critical ecosystems for human survival.

According to analysis of satellite data, tropical forests are being destroyed at a rate of at least 8 million hectares or 31,000 square miles a year. That's an area between the size of the Czech Republic and the United Arab Emirates that is chopped down every year. Brazil, Indonesia, the Democratic Republic of Congo and Malaysia had the highest rates of rainforest loss between 2012 and 2014.

That converts to roughly 54,000 acres of tropical rainforest that we are losing daily, along with additional degrading of forest on top of that. We are also losing other life at a rate of knots with 135 plant, animal and insect species being lost every day or 50,000 species a year, as the rainforests are destroyed.

Turning our beautiful and naturally diverse planet into a gigantic farm.

Why Should I Care About the Rainforests?

There's a reason the Amazon is known as the 'Lungs of the Planet' – it helps you and I to breathe.

When plants grow, they absorb atmospheric carbon into their tissues via the process of photosynthesis. Because rainforests are full of large trees and other plants, they store massive amounts of carbon. But when they are burned or chopped down, much of that carbon is released into the atmosphere as carbon dioxide and other greenhouse gases (nitrous oxide, methane, and other nitrogen oxides). The clearing and burning of tropical forests and peatlands accounts for about 10% of greenhouse gases from human activities.

Therefore, it is critical that we protect and restore rainforests to slow down climate change. It is estimated that the carbon absorbed by rainforests could offset as much as 50% of the release of fossil fuel carbon between now and 2050, preventing a 2 degree rise in global temperatures, so long as we stopped chopping them down!

Up in Flames 2019: the Amazon and Australia

Even though you may live nowhere near the Amazon, it is the world's largest carbon dioxide sink, estimated to capture 25% of global CO_2 generation. Without the Amazon, concentrations of CO2 would increase, global temperatures would rise along with sea levels, leading to catastrophe.

In 2019, fires in the Amazon increased by 80%, primarily brought on by deforestation for agriculture and logging. At one point, 7,000 square miles of the forest were in flames, an area just smaller than the size of New Jersey.

The government has encouraged more agricultural activity and development, forest protections and enforcement of illegal logging has weakened, leading to this huge loss of biodiversity, which affects the animals, local communities and ultimately ALL of us.

Once again, some humans are taking more than they need and upsetting the balance of life on this planet. Once the Amazon has gone, it's gone.

In Australia from September 2019 and well into February 2020, bushfires raged across the country, their worst ever. The amount of land affected across the country was more than 12.6 million hectares, which is comparable to the land area of England; 13 million hectares. It was estimated that the fires have emitted 434 million tonnes of carbon dioxide back into the atmosphere, 33 people died and over 1 billion animals were killed in the fires.

A hotter and drier climate over the past years has contributed to fires becoming more frequent and more intense. Many parts of Australia have been in drought conditions over the past few years, which has made it easier for fires to start and spread.

We are getting big bright warning signs from Mother Nature to encourage us to discontinue the path we have gone down, giving us glimpses into the chaos that will ensue if we don't change.

We're Feeding Animals Not Humans

We currently produce enough food to feed 10 billion people and the total supply of crops being currently fed to animals could feed at least 4 billion people.

One of the most ironic and disturbing facts is that in many parts of the world we have people that are starving, reaching 821 million in 2017, or one in every nine people. Yet in many industrialised countries, we are dying from excessive amounts of food, with more than one in eight adults in the world now obese. The problem is most significant in North America, but Africa and Asia are also experiencing an increase.

Undernutrition and obesity coexist in many countries and even in the same households, with poor access to nutritious food due to its higher cost, the stress of living with food scarcity, and the physical adaptations to food deprivation explaining why food-impoverished families may have a higher risk of obesity and being overweight.

Many of the top diseases we experience are also diet and lifestyle related, which means that they can be prevented and reversed, by making the right food choices.

I read counter articles all the time from well-meaning farmers of free-range/grass-fed cattle farms who state that going vegan is not the answer and that all this plant-based food production – namely soy crop monoculture farming – is the main cause of soil erosion, deforestation and environmental damage. Yet if we delve a little deeper as to why and who is actually consuming all the farmed soy, it's livestock animals not humans.

Protein-rich soy is such an important feed ingredient that the average European consumes approximately 61 kg of soy per year, largely indirectly through the animal products that they eat like chicken, pork, salmon, cheese, milk and eggs. If the global demand for animal products keeps growing, then it's estimated that soy production would need to increase by nearly 80% to feed all the animals being farmed for meat.

Soy is the largest source of protein for farmed animals, as it is cheap and effective in helping livestock reach market weight in record times. And don't forget that this feed is also fortified with additional vitamins and minerals to support this unnatural growth.

Soy is obviously associated with many meat-free, dairy-free and meat-replacement products, such as tofu, tempeh, soy milk, etc. but the bulk of the world's soy is not consumed by humans.

Feed crops are already produced in many of Earth's most valuable and vulnerable areas, such as the Amazon, Cerrado (Brazil), Congo Basin (Central Africa), Yangtze (China), Mekong (China, Myanmar (Burma), Thailand, Laos, Cambodia, and Vietnam), Himalayas and the Deccan Plateau (India) forests. These ecosystems are under growing pressure from the growth of farming and its need for feed, which threatens the biodiversity and natural resources in these areas.

We already eat much more animal protein than we need to lead healthy lives. In the UK the nutritional guidelines recommend 45–55 g of protein per day, and the average consumption is 64–88 g.

Although I would love everyone to shift to a plant-based diet overnight, it's not necessary to make an immediate impact. If most people who eat meat seven days a week were to cut down and eat it three days per week, while getting the rest of their protein requirements from plant-based sources, this would have a huge impact. And once you start scaling those behaviours up to millions and billions of people then we are in a position to really make a difference to our destiny. It's all about Progress not Perfection, with everyone contributing by living and eating responsibly.

Our habits are affecting the climate and the climate is affecting food security and nutrition on a global scale.

Global Greenhouse Gas Emissions

According to the UN, the livestock industry is responsible for 18% of global greenhouse gas emissions, while transportation exhaust is responsible for 13% of all greenhouse gas emissions. Then we can add on the additional fossil fuels needed to transport the livestock around the world.

The FAO (Food and Agriculture Organization of the United Nations) has been known to frequently undercount their statistics. In one report it states that 21.7 billion head of livestock were raised worldwide in 2002, while many non-governmental organisations report that about 50 billion head of livestock were raised each year in the early 2000s. Therefore if this is the case for many of the statistics, we could expect something much higher in terms of global greenhouse gas emissions from livestock.

And, in fact, another similar study was published by the Worldwatch Institute. They reassessed and found that uncounted, overlooked, and misallocated livestock-related GHG emissions came closer to 51% of all worldwide greenhouse gas emissions.

"Livestock and their by-products account for at least 32,000 million tons of carbon dioxide (CO_2) per year, or 51% of all worldwide greenhouse gas emissions."
The Worldwatch Institute

Now whatever the most accurate figure is, it lies somewhere between 18–51%, which either way you look at it is a huge proportion of emissions coming from just one industry.

Carbon dioxide is still the primary greenhouse gas, which research has shown contributes significantly to global warming. But methane is a close second coming from livestock, among others such as nitrous oxide and ozone.

While CO_2 persists in the atmosphere for centuries, or even millennia, methane warms the planet intensely for a decade or two before decaying to CO_2.

In those short decades, methane warms the planet by 86 times as much as CO_2, according to the Intergovernmental Panel on Climate Change (IPCC).

Globally, livestock are the largest source of methane from human-related activities.

CO_2 and Nutrient Quality

We've known for a while now about the heat-trapping and global warming effects of CO2, as more of it enters the atmosphere it causes temperatures to rise, ice caps to melt and sea levels to rise.

But It also has a huge effect on the nutrient quality of plant life. A study was conducted in 1998 at the Arizona State University in relation to zooplankton. They found that by shining light on algae it would grow much faster, which in turn should have led to an increase in the food supply for the zooplankton. But at a certain point, the zooplankton started struggling to survive, which didn't make sense to the scientists at the time, as they believed that an abundant food supply (algae) should have equalled an increase in zooplankton numbers.

The increased light was making the algae grow faster but was reducing the nutrient content of it. The zooplankton had plenty to eat, but their food was less nutritious. So they were starving of nutrients, not dissimilar to the current situation with our excessive amounts of food availability but reduced nutrient density, which has led us down the diet-related illness path.

Plants rely on both light and carbon dioxide to grow. If shining more light results in faster growing, less nutritious algae then it seemed logical to the Arizona lab scientists that ramping up carbon dioxide might do the same.

For the next 17 years, Irakli Loladze, a mathematician who had witnessed the initial experiment, poured over the scientific literature for any studies to support the theory and the results he collected pointed to the nutrient reducing effect they had learned about in the Arizona lab, and that it also appeared to be occurring in fields and forests around the world.

"Every leaf and every grass blade on Earth makes more and more sugars as CO_2 levels keep rising," Loladze said. "We are witnessing the greatest injection of carbohydrates into the biosphere in human history, an injection that dilutes other nutrients in our food supply."

The atmosphere is literally changing the nutrient quality of the food we eat, elevating CO_2 to the levels we are likely to experience in our lifetime which could drive down important minerals like calcium, potassium, zinc and iron by 8% on average.

Counter to the argument used by many politicians to debunk the global warming debate as a myth, sighting the fact that plants need carbon dioxide and that increased carbon dioxide in the atmosphere must be good for increasing plant/food growth, we now know that while it may increase the growth and yield, it reduces the nutrient quality. In this case, more does not equal better.

CO_2 and Pollen

Lewis Ziska, a plant physiologist at the Agricultural Research Service headquarters in Beltsville, Maryland, published a paper based on an experiment of how CO2 levels could affect goldenrod, a wildflower extremely important to bees.

Protein content of goldenrod pollen has declined by a third since the Industrial Revolution and this change correlates to the rise in CO_2.

For a long time now scientists have been looking into the cause of declining bee populations, as it threatens crop production that relies on the bees for pollination. The paper written by Lewis Ziska highlighted that the decline in protein before winter had set in could be a factor in reducing the bee's ability to fight off other challenges to their survival.

Experiments are also being performed on bell peppers to measure how vitamin C changes under elevated CO2, along with coffee to see whether caffeine declines under similar circumstances.

Plants are a crucial source of protein in the developing world due to their cost effectiveness, but by 2050, it is estimated that 1.4 billion people could be put at risk of protein deficiency.

This estimate includes 613.6 million people at risk in sub-Saharan Africa, 276.4 million in India, 131.7 million in Eastern and Southeast Asia and the Pacific, 84.4 million in Central Latin America and the Caribbean, and 77.8 million elsewhere in South Asia.

Let's now look at the crazy facts and chain of events that I have discussed in this chapter so far:

- Industrialised countries consume over twice as much meat as developing nations.
- The livestock industry produces between 18–51% of all global greenhouse gas emissions.
- Our rainforests, which we are destroying to grow livestock feed and graze cattle, could offset as much as 50% of CO_2 emissions, if they are not destroyed.
- Increased levels of CO2 are causing a reduction in nutrient density in plant foods and protein in pollen for bees.
- Plants are a crucial source of protein in the developing world.
- We currently grow enough food to feed 10 billion people.
- Livestock feed alone could feed 4 billion people.
- 821 million people are starving.
- By 2050, 1.4 BILLION people could be put at risk of protein deficiency.

We are literally creating all of our own problems and it's the top few percent of people in the world that can actually afford large quantities of the meat which is causing much of the problem for the atmosphere of our planet.

Imagine if billions of people just reduced their consumption, that would be a start.

Progress Not Perfection...

What if We All Went Plant Based?

I've heard the argument many times, 'well what would happen with all the animals if everyone went vegan? We'd be overrun with them!'

Like there would be a sudden cut-off overnight and when the clock strikes midnight everyone will stop eating meat. It wouldn't happen like that. People's habits change gradually, farmers would reduce the volume of animals being bred and farmed due to reduced demand and it would phase out gradually.

From what I've discussed in this chapter, many of the facts speak for themselves:

- Crops would be used to feed 4 million starving people rather than farmed animals.
- Pasture areas would be reduced by 80%, preventing the destruction of rainforests, 'the planets lungs', for use in cattle grazing and feed production.
- 18–50% reduction in global greenhouse gas emissions, slowing down global warming.
- We would avoid creating fishless ocean 'dead zones'.
- 74 billion land animals would avoid trauma, suffering and slaughter each year.

I often wonder if this would lead to a reduction of violence in our society?

We would save trillions globally on the treating of ill health caused by obesity, which is set to top $1.2tn every year from 2025. With less dairy, processed meats and junk food on the table, we would see a huge shift in people's health.

VEGAN MYTH BUSTING
EATING MEAT IS NATURAL

Unlike many hardcore vegans that believe we are natural herbivores, I believe that we are an omnivorous species, which has been proved.

Omnivores are naturally 'opportunistic feeders' and have the ability to consume both animal- and plant-derived foods to survive. We are neither totally carnivorous with rows of canine teeth and short digestive systems to cope with decaying flesh, but neither are we totally herbivorous with long digestive systems. Ours is smaller than a herbivore's and longer than a carnivore's, plus we produce hydrochloric acid for breaking down plant and animal matter, which herbivores do not.

It's this ability to be flexible with the source of our nutrients that has enabled our species to survive for so long, eating meat when there were no plants available and eating plants when there was no meat available, through the changing seasons on our planet. But this ability is a survival mechanism and just because we have done something in the past, it doesn't mean that it is applicable in the day and age we live in.

If you were living in the wild and had to survive through cold winters with little to no vegetation and had to hunt and kill to stay alive, then I would say you and I would eat anything to survive – to suggest otherwise is disingenuous and naïve – but the difference being that you would only take and eat what is necessary.

If you've bought this book on Amazon via a computer, iPhone or indeed drove to the book store to get a copy, then that would suggest you are not surviving but in fact thriving and that you most probably have access to a grocery store, supermarket and a decent selection of plant-based foods all year round.

There's nothing natural about the way we breed, feed, forcibly grow and traumatise farm animals for human consumption, maximising the speed of their growth to maximise profit and availability.

An animal is a living, breathing being that eats and shits just like us, but we have turned this sentient being into a commodity on a conveyor belt, that will likely not live beyond 10% of its actual life potential.

It gets imprisoned, tormented, killed, cut up and boxed up like its life didn't even exist, a mass-produced product in a factory. And with the population rising all the time, this is only going to get more unnatural than it already is, unless we change our habits and reduce the demand for it.

CHAPTER RECIPE

VEGAN MAC 'N' CHEESE

When you realise you can get Vegan Mac 'n' Cheese, you know everything is going to be alright.

This is one of those dishes that people feel they will miss out on when going vegan, but never fear, you won't look back once you taste this. Plus this is so much lighter than a traditional dairy-cheese version that would leave me feeling sick.

Servings: 2

Ingredients:

For the Béchamel/White Sauce:

- Aquafaba/chickpea water
- Non-dairy milk
- Grated vegan cheddar cheese (add 1 handful per person)
- 1 tbsp yeast flakes
- Pinch of salt
- 1 tsp of Dijon mustard

For the Pasta

- 100 g of macaroni gluten-free pasta per person.
- 200 g cherry tomatoes
- 1 clove fresh garlic
- Salt and pepper
- Extra virgin olive oil

You will need:

- 1 small pan for the béchamel sauce
- 1 large pan for pasta
- 1 small frying pan for cherry tomatoes
- 1 stirring spoon
- 1 baking dish for the bake
- 1 cheese grater

Cooking Method:

1. To make the sauce, stir and simmer all ingredients, add the non-dairy milk until you have a smooth custard like consistency.
2. Bring a pan of boiling water to the boil and add the pasta.
3. Pan fry cherry tomatoes with garlic, pinch of salt and pepper and olive oil.
4. Once the pasta is cooked, stir through with the cherry tomatoes etc.
5. Add the pasta mixture to a baking dish and pour over the white sauce, then grate more vegan cheese over the top to finish.
6. Oven bake at 200°C until golden and crispy on the top.

CHAPTER 24

THE VEGANS ARE COMING!

The rise of veganism has been explosive in the UK and around the world. One of the most interesting organisations that give us a measure of just how popular and how quickly the uptake has been is the charity 'Veganuary'. The organisation encourages people to sign up and pledge to go vegan in January, a perfect time for a new year's resolution and a perfect time as most people are sick of turkey, cheese and milk chocolate by then.

I went vegan back in 2014, the year that Veganuary was launched. The rise in just six years has been nothing short of meteoric. I've been conscious of the growth and interest just from my own perspective but seeing it in the figures below, really fills you with hope for the future.

In the six years since 2014, the campaign has gone from 3,300 participants to an incredible 400,000 in 2020; and even since I started writing this book in 2018 it has over doubled from 168k that year.

400,000 people signed up for the 2020 campaign. They estimated this represented the carbon dioxide equivalent of 450,000 flights and the lives of more than a million animals.

People from almost every country in the world signed up to try Veganuary in 2020.

The top ten countries were: United Kingdom, USA, Germany, Chile, Argentina, Mexico, Italy, South Africa, Australia and Sweden.

Over 80 celebrity ambassadors supported the campaign and gave veganism visibility.

The first Veganuary TV ad aired on major networks in five countries and was seen by millions around the world.

In 2020, health just pipped ethics to the post as the major driver for people taking part: health 38%, ethics 37%, environment 18% and other 7%.

The number of participants they have had since their inception in 2014 is even more incredible and a reflection of the rise in popularity of the plant-based movement and the increasing level of awareness in our society:

2014 – 3,300
2015 – 12,800
2016 – 23,000
2017 – 59,500
2018 – 168,500
2019 – 250,310
2020 – 400,000

These figures alone are proof that many people are starting to adopt a more conscious and compassionate way of living.

How Much Meat are we Eating Now?
In 2017, an estimated 29% of evening meals in Great Britain

did not contain meat or fish, according to a consumer research group. Government data also says households are buying less meat now.

As veganism goes more mainstream and becomes less of an extreme way of living, dispelling some of the old stereotypes surrounding the movement, it attracts the attention of a growing number of people, creating less barriers for entry. This is why I always recommend to people to lean into the movement, try it one day and see how you feel, it doesn't necessarily mean that you are then labelled a vegan for the rest of your life but it will open up a whole new world of food and ways of cooking for you. After all, life is about exploring and experiencing different things.

The funny thing is that if it feels good to you internally then you will naturally do more of it; there's no need to force it, just allow your internal compass to guide you.

Plant-Based News

Aside from the obvious growth shown with Veganuary's statistics, there are some other amazing signs that the plant-based movement is growing faster than ever before and is here to stay.

Another great platform where I get much of my plant-based news stories from is the media hub www.plantbasednews.org, who have their fingers on the pulse and provide a lot of fascinating industry stories, facts and figures, reporting on everything from food, to fashion, to sport, ethics, activism and the environment.

I was lucky enough to sit down and chat with Robbie Lockie from Plant Based News about how the organisation was started. It was initially founded as a YouTube channel by Klaus Mitchell to focus on a broad range of news topics relating to plant-based news.

In 2016, Robbie came on board and they created a website, acquired an editor and then out of the blue were contacted by Prince Khaled (bin Alwaleed bin Talal) from Saudi Arabia who offered to help fund the organisation. This has helped them develop and grow their team, allowing them to reach further around the globe, charting the growth of the whole movement around the world.

From 2017–2018, their audience has grown seven times in size, with their website pulling in-between 1.5 and 1.7 million unique visitors a month; and with google searches for vegan-related topics increasing 400% in the last few years it really does 'give you an idea of the growth the movement is currently witnessing.

In November 2019 they released their fifth annual high-quality hour-long feature film (2015–2019), and for the last two years have screened it at the Prince Charles Theatre in London, due to popularity, then releasing it on their YouTube channel later in the month.

Here's a brief overview of the rise of plant power in 2019:

- The world's leading scientists release a report that we have to change how we eat and grow food to fight climate change.
- The Amazon rainforest had an 84% increase in forest

fires causing global outrage.

- Greta Thunberg, the teenage climate activist, rose in fame and brought much global awareness to climate change.
- In the UK high street, baker Greggs released its vegan sausage roll. There was so much demand for it that they sold out, and it gave their profits a bumper 58% rise.
- The rise of Extinction Rebellion created global awareness of climate change with various protest across the world, shutting down cities gaining the attention of governments.
- Plant-based meat company Beyond Meat went public on the US stock market and its share price nearly tripled.
- Impossible Foods, also in the US, released their Impossible Burger in Burger King chains across the US.
- Plant-based tennis player Novak Djokovic won his fifth Wimbledon singles title.
- Plant-based Formula One driver Lewis Hamilton won his sixth World Championship.
- Highly anticipated documentary *The Game Changers* was released charting the success of plant-based athletes.
- I've seen at first hand a huge increase in people contacting me for plant-based advice and coaching after watching this film.
- The actor Joaquin Phoenix, who has been vegan for 40 years, won a Best Actor Oscar (2020) for his role in the film *Joker* and gave a powerful acceptance speech raising awareness of the cruelty of animal agriculture.

- Plant-based sales surged to $4.5 billion in the US.
- 700% increase in people following a plant-based diet in the last few years.
- Dairy-alternatives market projected to hit $14.36 billion by 2022.
- Dairy-free milk rose 6% and cows' milk dropped 3%.
- Vegan growth driving meat-alternative market to exceed $6 billion by 2023.
- UK vegan bacon brand raises £4.7 million after major growth.
- Plant-based meat market worth $27.9 billion by 2025.
- US oat milk sales surge by 686%.

Plant-Based Entrepreneurs

The increased popularity and demand for a plant-based diet has given rise to many new creative businesses, especially in the UK where vegan entrepreneurship is booming.

In 2018, the founders of the leading plant-based festival 'Vevolution' launched a specific Plant-based business bootcamp event, which reflected the need for more business guidance and creativity within the emerging market.

I sat down with the founders Damien and Judy to discuss.

What inspired you to launch Vevolution and specifically the plant-based business bootcamp?

We started Vevolution as we saw so many problems in the world that needed addressing – a climate crisis, health crisis, environment crisis and we've got a crisis with animals suffering – and we felt that there needed a platform where people could come and speak. We wanted to create an inclusive space for early-stage vegans, non-judgemental and where people felt safe to feel part of the movement to help them on the journey.

We were really inspired by TED talks and we felt that the plant-powered movement needed something to match, so that it would be taken more seriously outside of the vegan bubble, in amazing venues much like the BFI (British Film Institute) on London's Southbank where our last two events in 2018 and 2019 have taken place.

Our events are very different in that the focus is on inspirational and educational talks at the forefront. We do have food stalls and products but the focus is on the talks and panel discussions, with it all being very positive and solution-based, bringing people together to make a difference.

We started the plant-based business bootcamp as we are passionate about supporting entrepreneurs as we are entrepreneurs and Vevolution has become a hub for entrepreneurs and creativity, in London, the UK and across Europe.

We wanted to speak to plant-based entrepreneurs and not just give them business ideas but to also provide a support network of likeminded people following similar paths.

We also identified that it would have been a really valuable event for us when we first started Vevolution and wanted to help people avoid burnout and that feeling of being alone when you're on the path of an entrepreneur, especially as you don't have a big team of people to rely on and take the pressure off.

We also wanted to bring in businesses outside the plant-based world to help people expand their horizons.

How would you sum up the rise of vegan businesses?
Every year we sit down and say surely this year can't be as great for veganism as the year before, and every year it is. Our role is to help people in the mainstream understand that these business and services we are creating are for everyone, encouraging more people to eat more plants, even if you're not 100% vegan.

Plant-Based Restaurants
In 2016, Cem Yildiz and his co-founder Rojdan Gul launched 'What the Pitta', a vegan doner kebab restaurant, made with soy and marinated in a delicious but top-secret recipe, wrapped in a fresh tortilla made on site.

Cem was inspired to go vegan after visiting a local vegan café where he used to live in Chingford (northeast London) called 'The Feel Good Café'. He loved the food and felt compelled to learn more about the plant-based diet. He was then invited to watch a talk in London by Dr Michael Greger, the author of *How not to Die* and the nutrition website nutritionfacts.org. His talk spelled out for Cem the health benefits of a plant-based diet, and he soon realised that he needed to make the transition to a plant-based diet a permanent one.

It was during a holiday in Turkey with his soon-to-be

business partner Roj that 'What The Pitta' was born. After discussing his new vegan diet, Roj told him that his uncle had a successful vegan doner kebab business in Germany. Realising there was a gap in the market in London for something similar they decided to pay Roj's uncle a visit.

So as soon as they got back from their holiday, they booked flights to Germany and spent two to three days learning the secret recipe from Roj's uncle. On the journey home they secured the first location for their business, a small wooden food shack in Shoreditch, East London. Just two weeks after having the initial idea, 'What The Pitta' was born, and the rest is history.

They have now grown to six locations; three in London, one in Croydon, one in Brighton and one in Manchester, showing that the demand for vegan food outlets is really growing.

Erpingham House – The Biggest Plant-Based Restaurant in the UK

In 2018 entrepreneur Loui Blake launched 'Erpingham House' in a beautiful grade 2 listed building and as of writing is the UK's biggest plant-based restaurant located in Norwich, spanning several floors.

What inspired you to launch Erpingham House

I spent a lot of time in the US from 2016 - 2018 and was amazed by how accessible & delicious vegan food was in places like LA & New York. I knew that food is often the first thing people think of in going vegan, so by creating a food offering akin to those that had inspired me abroad, I could hope to inspire people in my home city & then in London to not only amend their food choices, but as a result make veganism desirable.

How would you sum up the rise of your businesses and veganism?
I certainly think my timing has helped in establishing Erpingham House. The word vegan is popping up more and more, and we're seeing more people choose to eat food free from animal products even if they wouldn't consider themselves vegan. Of course, I believe we're still very early, but i think it's a great time to have a business in this space.

In early 2020 Loui opened a second Erpingham House location in Brighton.

Plant-Powered Partying
There is a definite correlation between this vegan journey and a raising of consciousness and awareness to other global and health issues. In London especially, people are looking for a new way to party. They are not happy working five days a week only to then drink themselves into oblivion for two nights, dealing with the hangovers that follow, only to go back to work and do it all again on Monday. Surely there's a way of having fun and raising your energetic vibration rather than destroying it?

It's not just the food side of the plant-based movement which is witnessing a surge. London is seeing a demand for more conscious partying, with no alcohol and no drugs policies for popular parties such as 'Morning Gloryville' which launched in 2013, catering for early morning ravers, who want to exercise, dance and have fun before going to work. It offers sober ravers hot cacao, and a variety of different smoothies and snacks, all plant based, and a space to go crazy with other likeminded souls raising each other's energy through ecstatic dancing.

'Rise and Shine Parties' is another party founded by vegan model, events and community creator Anthony Lowther. Rise and Shine is also alcohol and drug free but super food elixirs and smoothies are IN. They get you rocking with natural energy without the hangover at the end. The events are loads of fun and filled with incredible energy from amazing likeminded people. I've been along to many of the events and get so engrossed in the energy that I always dance my ass off, leaving the party feeling better than when I arrived.

Rise and Shine also held their first three festival weekend retreats in 2019 with more planned in the future, once the Covid-19 global pandemic has passed.

The Plant Based Games

I took part in the first team-based Plant Based Games in London, 2019. The Plant Based Games is a team and individual cross-fit style competition created purely for vegan athletes and was the brainchild of London based fitness professionals; Connor McDonald, Sammy Harper, and William Brown to raise awareness for the plant-based movement and the positive performance benefits that come with a vegan diet. They have since held a competition in 2020 and have another planned for 2021.

Social Proof

Nothing is certain in this day and age but we can definitely see from all the social proof above that a more conscious side to society in the UK is rising, and all evidence suggests that the plant-based movement is growing faster than ever before. The term veganism is gradually shedding some of the more negative connotations it has had historically, reducing the barriers of entry and making it accessible and enticing for people wishing to try something new, who are ready to change.

With the mainstream media now willing to discuss veganism and its merits on their platforms, it has opened a whole new arena of discussion that is the start of a long journey towards a more conscious future for humanity.

Meat from Labs not Animals

Cultured meat offers a way to potentially grow infinite portions of meat from just a handful of cells in a laboratory. Under the right conditions in a lab, cells can be encouraged to divide just like they do inside the body, thus cutting down on natural resources, gas and of course the trauma and suffering to the animals farmed for consumption, as the cells only need to be taken once from an animal to start the culture.

There are many new 'clean meat' companies getting huge investments which will bring the production costs down. In 2013, producing the first lab-grown burger cost $325,000. By 2015, the cost had dropped to around $11 and the first 'cultured' or 'clean meat', produced from animal cells without an actual animal, may be in restaurants in the next few years.

Not only could the 'clean meat' industry start the shift away from killing animals and damaging our environment, but it could also replace part of the economy and livelihoods for those in the agriculture industry rather than wiping it out, as farmers could in the future begin to shift from animal agriculture to cellular agriculture.

It won't overtake traditional farming methods anytime soon but alongside the growth of the plant-based movement, it can share the environmental burden, as the world adapts to a growing demand for meat using traditional methods of animal agriculture that strain the environment.

I would of course love to see people shift away entirely from eating 'farmed' meat in any shape or form, as it would remove the need for this entirely but not everyone is ready to give up their meat eating. And let's face it, no one actually eats meat to intentionally kill an animal, we eat meat for the rich flavours, colours, textures and of course traditions, so as long as the source of the meat is tasty, healthy, and cost effective, should people really be concerned whether it comes from an animal or a lab?

It may sound a bit 'Frankenstein' to some people, and a weird science experiment that could go wrong, but surely it is better than the current daily 'genocide' that we put farmed animals through?

Is your longing for flavour, texture and tradition worth more than the life, trauma and suffering of a sentient being?

CHAPTER RECIPE

BARLEY BUDDHA BOWL

I thought it was fitting to end this chapter with a delicious and nutritious simple recipe that encompasses one of the main principles of Buddhism, the principle of equality: that all living entities are equal.

This one pot wonder is full of flavour, texture, colour and is quick and simple to make, enjoy!

Servings: 1–2 depending on hunger levels!

Ingredients:

- 100 g tempeh
- 80 g pearled barley
- 1 handful peas
- 1 handful broccoli
- 1 handful rainbow chard
- 1 handful of broccoli sprouts
- 1 small handful of chopped fresh dill
- 1 red onion sliced finely
- 1 fresh clove of garlic chopped finely
- 1 tbsp dark miso
- ½ lemon
- 1 big handful of empathy and compassion

You will need:

- 1 pan for boiling water
- 1 large frying pan for the main dish
- 1 griddle pan or smaller frying pan for the tempeh

'rashers'

- 1 sharp knife
- 1 chopping board
- 1 wooden stirring spoon

Cooking Method:

1. Bring a pan of water to the boil, add the barley and leave to cook for 20–25 minutes.
2. Then sauté the onion and garlic in a large frying pan (preferably with a lid) with a little coconut oil and water. This will help to soften and cook them without sticking to the pan. Place the lid on for a couple of minutes.
3. Then add the peas, broccoli, rainbow chard and the dark miso, along with a little more water to help steam the vegetables and dilute the miso, creating a bit of a sauce.
4. Slice the tempeh into rasher-style pieces, toss them in a little tamari and olive oil then griddle or pan fry them on each side until crispy. Be careful not to burn.
5. Add the barley to the mixture in the large frying pan and stir through with the sprouts, chopped dill and the juice of half a squeezed lemon, then serve with the crispy tempeh on top.

CHAPTER 25

THE CHOICE IS (Y)OURS

"Eventually everyone sits down to
a banquet of consequences."
Robert Louis Stevenson

On October 8th 2018, a report from UN Scientists on the Intergovernmental Panel of Climate Change (IPCC) was released stating that the world has 10–12 years to get climate change under control. Then one year later the IPCC released another report stating that we have to change how we eat and grow food to fight climate change.

This makes the message in this book even more timely and important to me, and to you and to all of us as guardians of the planet.

I want to reduce the trauma and suffering that I leave in the wake of my life on this planet, improving the quality of life rather than reducing it or destroying it completely. I hope now after reading this book and seeing things through my eyes and words that you also feel compelled to reduce the trauma and suffering that your life leaves behind.

Unlike many other species that we share this planet with, human beings have been gifted the ability to make conscious choices. We are obviously also governed by our genetic nature and desires, but ultimately we have the ability to have an internal dialogue, weighing up the pros and cons before we act.

This 'gift' or 'curse' has enabled us to create incredible technologies and to advance us as a species in so many miraculous directions. But it has also given us the belief that we are above nature, better than nature, almost god-like, believing that we don't have the need to work with nature but will force nature to do our own bidding. This of course is where everything has started to unravel for us.

Other species on our planet only ever take what they need to survive. Because for other species survival is their goal (there may be only one or two exceptions to this rule). We, on the other hand, have created many different goals in life for ourselves to pursue, that give our lives additional meaning above the need for survival and unfortunately as soon as we start looking beyond the basic needs for food, shelter, water and relationships, we start to consume more than we should and the natural balance of life is thrown out.

Unfortunately, farmers themselves sometimes cull certain species of animals such as rabbits and foxes to protect their animals, crops and their livelihoods from being drained of all resources when these species start breeding out of control. Human beings have now bred out of control and are draining the world's natural resources.

Mother Nature is our farmer and if we don't start taking responsibility for our own conscious choices and decisions, then Mother Nature will no doubt start culling human beings, creating an inhospitable environment that will make it difficult for many people to survive.

If we know that we can not only survive but thrive on a plant-based diet, we can build muscle, improve performance, optimise our health and heal many diseases while also reducing our impact on the natural environment around us, then it's about time we start acting on our conscious thoughts and start being the change we wish to see in the world.

We each make at least three food choices every day – that's over one thousand food choices we all make individually each year. You could probably double that for those in the fitness and bodybuilding worlds.

If just 1 million people made 1,000 different food choices each year, that would be over 1 billion positive food choices made, thus having a huge impact on our environment. Now scale that to 1 billion people or several billion people then we are really in a position of power to positively affect the destiny of our species.

If 1 million people read this book, then that is potentially 1 billion positive food choices that will now be made.

We all have more power individually than we are led to believe, change always starts within us individually, from a thought, an idea, then an action. But we can't do this alone, we must do this together, because together in our numbers we really can be the change we wish to see in the world.

In this book I have given you evidence from my own experience, my body and my journey, the basic fundamental science and behavioural changes required for body transformation, along with the cold hard facts of how our food choices effect more than just our own immediate environments. I have proved that there is another choice on the table, and it is just as effective and beneficial for your health and our planet – it may be even better – and it is a choice that is available to us all.

You really can have a fit, healthy, strong and beautiful body by eating plants not animals, and you really can transform YOUR body and OUR planet, but only you can make that choice.

CHAPTER RECIPE

PLANT-POWERED POT NOODLE

This is a super quick, tasty and nutritious pot noodle soup. Just prepare all the fresh ingredients beforehand, throw it all into a lock tight container and when you're ready to eat just add hot water, let the noodles soak and soften, stir all the flavours around and you are good to go!

For a more Thai-flavoured dish, just add a drop of coconut milk when you're ready to eat and stir through.

Servings: 1

Ingredients:

- 2 fresh spring onions chopped
- 150 g organic non-GMO tofu
- 1 tbsp nutritional yeast flakes with B12
- 1 portobello mushroom chopped into small cubes
- 1 heaped tsp dark miso paste
- 1 serving vermicelli rice noodles
- 1 small bunch of chopped Thai basil or coriander
- ½ inch fresh ginger sliced into matchsticks
- ½ fresh garlic clove finely chopped
- ½ sweet red pepper
- ½ tsp sesame oil

You will need:

- 1 sharp knife
- 1 chopping board
- 1 sealable flask or lock tight Tupperware

- 1 spoon to eat

Cooking Method:

1. Prepare and add all the ingredients into a bowl or container ready to transport with you.
2. When you're ready just add boiling water, stir properly and put a lid over to leave for about 3–5 minutes until the noodles are soft.
3. Stir thoroughly to make sure the miso paste has dissolved, add the yeast flakes and enjoy!

CHAPTER 26

FURTHER RESOURCES

To help further support your plant-based journey I have added some of my favourite resources, so that you can learn more and build your network and community of support and information.

The movement is growing so fast now that there will be hundreds of new resources available after this book is published, so use Google and explore!

You are not alone...

Documentaries

The Game Changers – *http://gamechangersmovie.com*
Land of Hope and Glory - *https://www.landofhopeandglory.org*
Dominion – *http://watch.dominionmovement.com*
Running for Good – *https://runningforgoodfilm.com*
Vegan 2018 – *https://www.youtube.com/plantbasednews*
What The Health – *http://www.whatthehealthfilm.com*
Cowspiracy – *http://www.cowspiracy.com*
Forks Over Knives – *https://www.forksoverknives.com/*
Earthlings – *http://www.nationearth.com/*

Books

Plant Based Nutrition 2E (Idiot's Guide) by Julieanna Hever & Raymond Cronise
How Not to Die by Michael Greger
How to Create a Vegan World by Tobias Leenaert

Proteinaholic by Garth Davis
How to Go Vegan by Veganuary
Finding Ultra by Rich Roll
Eat and Run by Scott Jurek

Cookbooks

The Happy Pear
The Oh She Glows Cookbook
Thugs Kitchen
The Plantpower Way
This Cheese is Nuts

Web resources

My newsletter and blog *http://theplantpoweredpt.com*
Nutrition facts *http://NutritionFacts.org*
Plant-based doctor *https://drjoelkahn.com*
Charity and magazine *https://www.viva.org.uk*
Charity – Go Vegan in January *https://veganuary.com*
Plant-based Events *http://www.vevolution.co*
Vegan news website *https://www.plantbasednews.org*
The Vegan Society *https://vegansociety.com*
Podcast *http://www.richroll.com*
Podcast and plant-based fitness education:
http://www.nomeatathlete.com/
Fiona Oakes Animal Sanctuary
http://www.towerhillstables.com/

REFERENCES

Part 2

Food Alone May Not Provide Sufficient Micronutrients for Preventing Deficiency
https://jissn.biomedcentral.com/articles/10.1186/1550-2783-3-1-51

How and Why Too Much Protein Triggers Aging and Cancer
https://articles.mercola.com/sites/articles/archive/2016/05/07/too-much-protein-triggers-aging-cancer.aspx

Low Protein Intake is Associated with a Major Reduction in IGF-1, Cancer, and Overall Mortality in the 65 and Younger but Not Older Population
https://www.ncbi.nlm.nih.gov/pmc/articles/PMC3988204/

Antioxidants in Fruits
https://www.webmd.com/diet/features/antioxidants-in-fruits

Insulin and cortisol promote leptin production in cultured human fat cells.
https://www.ncbi.nlm.nih.gov/pubmed/8826983

High glycemic index carbohydrate diet alters the diurnal rhythm of leptin but not insulin concentrations.
https://www.ncbi.nlm.nih.gov/pubmed/11743140

Effects of short-term carbohydrate or fat overfeeding on energy expenditure and plasma leptin concentrations in healthy female subjects.
https://www.ncbi.nlm.nih.gov/pubmed/11126336

The role of lactate in the exercise-induced human growth hormone response: evidence from McArdle disease
https://www.ncbi.nlm.nih.gov/pubmed/18184755

The exercise-induced growth hormone response in athletes.
https://www.ncbi.nlm.nih.gov/pubmed/12797841

The Protein-Combining Myth
https://nutritionfacts.org/video/the-protein-combining-myth/

Effects of stress and injury on meat and by-product quality
http://www.fao.org/docrep/003/x6909e/x6909e04.htm

Stress hormones, carcass composition and meat quality in Large White Duroc pigs.
https://www.ncbi.nlm.nih.gov/pubmed/22063148

Antibiotics Overuse in Animal Agriculture: A Call to Action for Health Care Providers
https://www.ncbi.nlm.nih.gov/pmc/articles/PMC4638249/

Are Hormones in Meat Affecting Humans?
https://www.livestrong.com/article/464430-are-hormones-in-meat-affecting-humans/

Living Longer by Reducing Leucine Intake
https://nutritionfacts.org/2015/06/16/living-longer-by-reducing-leucine-intake/

mTOR-what does it do?
https://www.ncbi.nlm.nih.gov/pubmed/19100909

Cobalt deficiency in sheep and cattle
https://www.agric.wa.gov.au/livestock-biosecurity/cobalt-deficiency-sheep-and-cattle

Cobalt Deficiency in Sheep
https://www.farmhealthonline.com/disease-management/sheep-diseases/cobalt-deficiency-in-sheep/

Stop wasting vitamins, trace minerals in animal feeds
https://www.wattagnet.com/articles/25696-stop-wasting-vitamins-trace-minerals-in-animal-feeds

Vitamins and minerals: Essential for ruminants
https://www.allaboutfeed.net/Feed-Additives/Articles/2018/3/Vitamins-and-minerals-Essential-for-ruminants-256655E/

Vitamin B12 – Properties and Metabolism
https://www.dsm.com/markets/anh/en_US/Compendium/swine/vitamin_B12.html

Iron consumption can increase risk for heart disease, study shows
https://www.sciencedaily.com/releases/2014/04/140423170903.htm

Heme Iron, Zinc, Alcohol Consumption, and Colon Cancer: Iowa Women's Health Study
https://academic.oup.com/jnci/article/96/5/403/2521151

How to Increase Cell Volume for Fast Muscle Growth
https://www.t-nation.com/supplements/increase-cell-volume-for-fast-muscle-growth

Plant-Based Diets for Cardiovascular Safety and Performance in Endurance Sports
https://www.ncbi.nlm.nih.gov/pmc/articles/PMC6356661/

Part 3

Agriculture and Livestock Remain Major Sources of Greenhouse Gas Emissions
http://www.worldwatch.org/agriculture-and-livestock-remain-major-sources-greenhouse-gas-emissions-0

Livestock and Climate Change
http://www.worldwatch.org/files/pdf/Livestock%20and%20Climate%20Change.pdf

Sources and Resources for "Livestock and Climate Change"
http://www.worldwatch.org/ww/livestock

How much meat do we eat?
https://fullfact.org/health/vegetarian-vegan-uk/

Almost A Third Of Meals Are Now Vegetarian As Brits Cut Down On Meat
https://www.huffingtonpost.co.uk/entry/almost-a-third-

of-meals-are-now-vegetarian-as-brits-cut-down-on-meat_uk_5a7ada7de4b06505b4e9bf92

World Population Clock
http://www.theworldcounts.com/counters/shocking_environmental_facts_and_statistics/world_population_clock_live

How Many People Can Earth Support?
https://www.livescience.com/16493-people-planet-earth-support.html

Meat, Poultry & Seafood Market Size Worth $7.3 Trillion By 2025: Grand View Research, Inc.
https://www.prnewswire.com/news-releases/meat-poultry--seafood-market-size-worth-73-trillion-by-2025-grand-view-research-inc-683844731.html

Livestock a major threat to environment
http://www.fao.org/newsroom/en/News/2006/1000448/index.html

The Triple Whopper Environmental Impact of Global Meat Production
http://science.time.com/2013/12/16/the-triple-whopper-environmental-impact-of-global-meat-production/

We Already Grow Enough Food for 10 Billion People... and Still Can't End Hunger
https://www.commondreams.org/views/2012/05/08/we-already-grow-enough-food-10-billion-people-and-still-cant-end-hunger

A Global Assessment of the Water Footprint of Farm Animal Products
http://waterfootprint.org/media/downloads/Mekonnen-Hoekstra-2012-WaterFootprintFarmAnimalProducts.pdf

10 Rainforest Facts for 2018
https://rainforests.mongabay.com/facts/rainforest-facts.html

Rainforests could provide half global climate solution by 2050
https://news.mongabay.com/2015/11/forest-conservation-could-provide-half-global-climate-solution-by-2050/

Measuring the Daily Destruction of the World's Rainforests
https://www.scientificamerican.com/article/earth-talks-daily-destruction/

Appetite for Destruction
https://www.wwf.org.uk/sites/default/files/2017-10/WWF_AppetiteForDestruction_Summary_Report_SignOff.pdf

See how much of the Amazon is burning, how it compares to other years
https://www.nationalgeographic.com/environment/2019/08/amazon-fires-cause-deforestation-graphic-map/

Australia fires: A visual guide to the bushfire crisis
https://www.bbc.com/news/world-australia-50951043

The size of Australia's bushfire crisis captured in five big numbers
https://www.abc.net.au/news/science/2020-03-05/bushfire-crisis-five-big-numbers/12007716

Global hunger continues to rise, new UN report says
http://www.fao.org/news/story/en/item/1152031/icode/

Food Security & Nutrition around the World
http://www.fao.org/state-of-food-security-nutrition/en/

FAO – Livestock's Long Shadow
http://www.fao.org/docrep/010/a0701e/a0701e00.HTM

Worldwatch Institute - Livestock and Climate Change
http://www.worldwatch.org/files/pdf/Livestock%20and%20Climate%20Change.pdf

How Bad of a Greenhouse Gas Is Methane?
https://www.scientificamerican.com/article/how-bad-of-a-greenhouse-gas-is-methane/

The Great Nutrient Collapse
https://www.politico.com/agenda/story/2017/09/13/food-nutrients-carbon-dioxide-000511

Climate change will make hundreds of millions more people nutrient deficient
https://www.theguardian.com/science/2018/aug/27/climate-change-will-make-hundreds-of-millions-more-people-nutrient-deficient

Estimated Effects of Future Atmospheric CO2 Concentrations on Protein Intake and the Risk of Protein Deficiency by Country and Region
https://ehp.niehs.nih.gov/doi/10.1289/EHP41

Global cost of obesity-related illness to hit $1.2tn a year from 2025
https://www.theguardian.com/society/2017/oct/10/treating-obesity-related-illness-will-cost-12tn-a-year-from-2025-experts-warn

Veganuary Statistics
https://veganuary.com/blog/a-record-breaking-veganuary-2018/

How much meat do we eat?
https://fullfact.org/health/vegetarian-vegan-uk/

Almost A Third Of Meals Are Now Vegetarian As Brits Cut Down On Meat
https://www.huffingtonpost.co.uk/entry/almost-a-third-of-meals-are-now-vegetarian-as-brits-cut-down-on-meat_uk_5a7ada7de4b06505b4e9bf92

Lab-grown meat is coming, whether you like it or not
https://www.wired.com/story/lab-grown-meat/

Lab-grown meat is getting cheap enough for anyone to buy
https://www.fastcompany.com/40565582/lab-grown-meat-is-getting-cheap-enough-for-anyone-to-buy

The world has just over a decade to get climate change

under control, U.N. scientists say
https://www.washingtonpost.com/energy-environment/2018/10/08/world-has-only-years-get-climate-change-under-control-un-scientists-say/?utm_term=.517f32ee425f

Intergovernmental Panel on Climate Change (IPCC)
https://www.ipcc.ch/

Report: we have to change how we eat and grow food to fight climate change
https://www.vox.com/2019/8/8/20758461/climate-change-report-2019-un-ipcc-land-food

Plant-based Meat Market worth $27.9 billion by 2025
https://www.marketsandmarkets.com/PressReleases/plant-based-meat.asp

UK Vegan Bacon Brand Raises £4.7 Million After Major Growth
https://www.plantbasednews.org/lifestyle/vegan-bacon-brand-4-7-million

US Oat Milk Sales Surge By 686%
https://www.plantbasednews.org/lifestyle/us-oat-milk-sales-surge-686

Vegan Growth Driving Meat-Alternative Market To Exceed $6 Billion By 2023
https://www.plantbasednews.org/lifestyle/vegan-growth-driving-meat-alternative-market-to-exceed-6-billion-by-2023

Printed in Great Britain
by Amazon

58045869R00200